# TAROT
## HEALER

## About the Author

Leeza Robertson is the author of *Tarot Court Cards for Beginners* and *Tarot Reversals for Beginners*, and she's the creator of two tarot decks, the *Mermaid Tarot* and *Animal Totem Tarot*. When she doesn't have her nose inside a book or her fingers dancing across a deck of cards, she runs her online class with her business partner, Pamela Chen. Together they are the head witches at the High Vibe Tarot Academy, which you can find at bit.ly/uftamagic.

## To Write to the Author

If you wish to contact the author or would like more information about this book, please write to the author in care of Llewellyn Worldwide Ltd. and we will forward your request. Both the author and the publisher appreciate hearing from you and learning of your enjoyment of this book and how it has helped you. Llewellyn Worldwide Ltd. cannot guarantee that every letter written to the author can be answered, but all will be forwarded. Please write to:

Leeza Robertson
⁒ Llewellyn Worldwide
2143 Wooddale Drive
Woodbury, MN 55125-2989

Please enclose a self-addressed stamped envelope for reply,
or $1.00 to cover costs. If outside the U.S.A., enclose
an international postal reply coupon.

Many of Llewellyn's authors have websites with additional information and resources. For more information, please visit our website at http://www.llewellyn.com.

# TAROT
## HEALER

USING
the CARDS to
DEEPEN YOUR
### Chakra
### Healing
### Work

## LEEZA ROBERTSON

Llewellyn Publications
Woodbury, Minnesota

FIRST EDITION
Third Printing, 2021

Book design by Samantha Penn
Cover design by Shannon McKuhen
Cover illustration by Rebekah Nichols
Figure illustration on page 5 by Mary Ann Zapalac

Llewellyn Publications is a registered trademark of Llewellyn Worldwide Ltd.

**Library of Congress Cataloging-in-Publication Data**
Names: Robertson, Leeza, author.
Title: Tarot healer : using the cards to deepen your chakra healing work /
    Leeza Robertson.
Description: First edition. | Woodbury, Minnesota : Llewellyn Publications,
    2020. | Includes bibliographical references. | Summary: "Combining
    chakra healing techniques with the healing energy of tarot, Tarot Healer
    guides you through each of your seven chakras, showing you how to
    enhance your energy, find and clear blocks, and become your own tarot
    healer"— Provided by publisher.
Identifiers: LCCN 2020013655 (print) | LCCN 2020013656 (ebook) | ISBN
    9780738763767 (paperback) | ISBN 9780738764153 (ebook)
Subjects: LCSH: Tarot. | Chakras. | Energy medicine.
Classification: LCC BF1879.T2 R6132 2020  (print) | LCC BF1879.T2  (ebook)
    | DDC 133.3/2424--dc23
LC record available at—ttps://lccn.loc.gov/2020013655
LC ebook record available at https://lccn.loc.gov/2020013656

Llewellyn Publications
A Division of Llewellyn Worldwide Ltd.
2143 Wooddale Drive
Woodbury, MN 55125-2989
www.llewellyn.com

Printed in the United States of America

## Also by Leeza Robertson

*Animal Totem Tarot* (art by Eugene Smith)

*Mermaid Tarot* (art by Julie Dillon)

*Pathworking the Tarot*

*Tarot Court Cards for Beginners*

*Tarot Reversals for Beginners*

This book is dedicated to the lightworkers and earth angels. I see you and I thank you for your service.

## Acknowledgments

It takes a village to put a book into the marketplace, and this book would never have seen the light of day without my little village. Thank you to all the Llewellyn staff who made this book what it is today, with special thanks to Barbara Moore for always believing in my crazy ideas. A huge thank-you to my editors, Laure and Lauryn, who take my raw words and polish them to become sparkling gems. Most importantly, thank you, dear readers, because without you buying my books, I would not be able to keep writing them. And a heartfelt thanks to my wife, my biggest cheerleader and constant support person.

## Disclaimer

This book is not intended to provide medical or mental health advice or to take the place of advice and treatment from your primary care provider. Readers are advised to consult their doctors or other qualified healthcare professionals regarding the treatment of their medical or mental health problems. Neither the publisher nor the author take any responsibility for any possible consequences from any treatment to any person reading or following the information in this book.

# Contents

# Introduction

Many years ago, I started combining tarot with my work as an energy healing coach. What I noticed was that my clients were getting a deeper and more practical map to their healing journey, and so was I. The tarot allowed them and me to see their health, thoughts, feelings, and actions in new and profound ways. Not only did they have a visual reference to their current state of health, but they also had a visual map of the next steps in their energy healing journey. This can be just what a person needs to make a lifelong shift in how they see themselves and their bodies. Over the years, I have worked tarot even more deeply into my energy healing practice. I started using cards as healing significators and started using spreads to map out specific healing journeys, especially those within the chakras. The system of the tarot allows itself to be beautifully interwoven into healing work. The three parts of the tarot can be used as tools to view the three main aspects of healing work. The majors can represent the issue, and the court cards can represent how a person is working through that issue and who they may become once they have moved on to the next phase in the healing journey. The remaining cards, the minors, can map out daily habits, small actions, and emotional and mental programing needed for the person to, for instance, move from an old, out-dated illness story into a new, updated health and well-being story. Tarot has become such an integral part of my coaching practice that it seemed the next logical step was to put all that information into a book and share it with other people who wish to integrate tarot into their energy healing journey.

Think of this book as a self-study course, one that combines the energetic healing work of the chakra system with the healing energy of the tarot, and although this is not your normal tarot book, you will have plenty of fun with the cards along the way and may even learn a few ways to read the cards differently. This book, in essence, is a book to add to both your energy healing library and your tarot resource library. It is a book that takes you on a journey through your seven chakras and helps you get to know yourself and your body better.

This book will explore the tarot cards in both upright and reversed aspects, and you will see how each of these aspects has a deeper healing message for you and your healing journey. Even if you are not very comfortable with reversed cards, I urge you to stick with the reversed card exercises in this book. For the sake of this energy work, there are no good or bad positions for your cards, only information. This information will assist you along your energy healing path by showing you where you might be blocked, where you might have placed yourself into a protective state, and where you might need to deal with your shadow aspects. That might mean that you have to take your time with the content inside the pages of this book. It may also mean you find yourself not wanting to do some of the exercises and instead deeply drawn to others. All of this is normal on a healing journey. We don't always feel good about every step we take along the healing path. The key is to take your time, be kind and compassionate with yourself, and know when to dive more deeply or when you are not ready to look under the surface. Above all, don't label anything that presents itself on this journey as good or bad; it just is what it is, until it isn't anymore. This book is going to show you how you can become your own tarot healer, and by that I mean how to confidently interweave tarot, as an integral tool, with your own energy healing work.

Let's just get one thing straight: This is not a medical book, does not provide a medical diagnosis, and is by no means meant to stop you from seeking proper and informed medical care and assistance. This is a book that will help you to become better aware of how your thoughts, feelings, and actions impact the seven energy centers of your body. In my own work with clients, we use some of the processes I am sharing with you in this book alongside their medical plans. I am not a doctor, nor do I give out medical advice, so please know that this book is just another tool for your personal self-healing and overall well-being. It is, however, meant to be used in unison with your current energy healing practice, whatever that may be.

## The Tarot Healer Path

With that out of the way, who or what is a tarot healer? In reality this book is more of a gateway to working as an energy healer with a very strong integration of tarot in your work. This is not a certification program nor a cure-all. It doesn't matter what sort of energy work you do—incorporating elements from this book will deepen your practice. Tarot in and of itself is a very powerful healing tool if you know how to use it correctly. The cards open the door to deep physiological, emotional, spiritual, and physical exploration. All these things affect our overall health and well-being. A healer, in my humble opinion, is someone who holds space for healing energy to shift and flow and is a facilitator, if you will, to help change what happens in the body, mind, and spirit. For the sake of this book, I want to add that a tarot healer is someone who uses all the above to work with their energy via their seven chakras. Tarot healing is a way of exploring how to dialogue with, shift, and release thoughts, feelings, or beliefs that may actually be standing in the way of overall health and well-being or causing pain and suffering. This book gives one a map of how to use the tarot in conjunction with the seven chakras. It shows, in a very systematic way, how to go into each energy center and explore them with the cards of the tarot, and each chapter ends with a guided energy healing session using a tarot mandala.

There is a lot more to healing work than the medical side. Perceptions and beliefs play a massive role in our overall health and well-being, and tarot is incredibly helpful in identifying and strategizing with these two very important healing mindsets.

## Exploring the Chakras

All my energy healing work is chakra-based, and the chakras are the only system I personally work with. There is so much to learn from the chakra system, so much we really don't understand, and so many deep issues to explore within these energy centers. I have been working with the chakras on myself and others for over ten years, and the more I know about these magical spinning wheels of energy, the deeper my learning becomes. It is like there are layers within layers inside the chakras, and just as you become comfortable and confident with the layers, you burst through into another new layer of understanding.

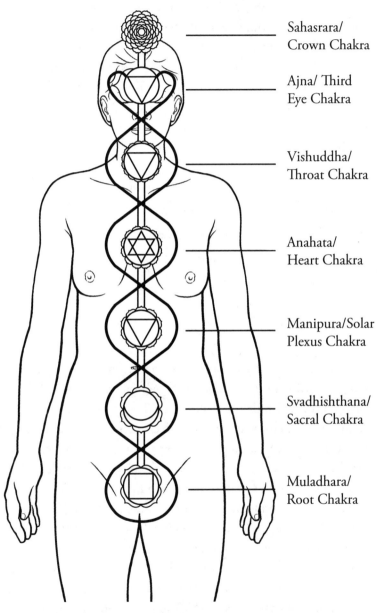

Sahasrara/
Crown Chakra

Ajna/ Third
Eye Chakra

Vishuddha/
Throat Chakra

Anahata/
Heart Chakra

Manipura/Solar
Plexus Chakra

Svadhishthana/
Sacral Chakra

Muladhara/
Root Chakra

So, what are chakras? Chakras, in very basic terms, are spinning energy centers that run through the body. There are seven main ones and hundreds of smaller ones. For the sake of this book, we are only going to focus on the seven main energy centers, their roles, the issues and concerns they govern, and how the tarot will assist you in getting to know your chakra system better so that you can harness your chakra energy for improved health and well-being.

The seven primary chakras are as follows:

- *Chakra 1:* Muladhara/Root
- *Chakra 2:* Svadhishthana/Sacral
- *Chakra 3:* Manipura/Solar Plexus
- *Chakra 4:* Anahata/Heart
- *Chakra 5:* Vishuddha/Throat
- *Chakra 6:* Ajna/Third Eye
- *Chakra 7:* Sahasrara/Crown

The first seven chapters in this book focus on one primary chakra, starting from the root, or the bottom chakra, working up through the sacral, the solar plexus, the heart, the throat, and the third eye to the crown at the top. Each chapter is broken down into seven sections, which outline the seven main issues each particular chakra deals with. You will notice the power of seven running through every aspect of this book, including seven chakras, seven sections, and the odd seven-card spread. Seven is the number of lessons and learning, and it is the number we associate with both the student and the master. This is what your journey as a tarot healer will feel like. There will be times when you will be humbled and feel very much like a student. Then there will be times when you will feel like you have some level of success and attainment, enough to share your experience with others. The energy of the seven even runs through the tarot, especially in telling of the Fool's journey, in which we break the majors up into three rows of seven cards. The power of the seven reminds us that we are in a constant lesson, always learning more about who we are, what we are capable of, and how we engage with our physical and vibrational being. As you make your way through this book, you will notice that these lessons are evident in the chakra work and the tarot.

Let's take a closer look at the role tarot plays in this book. There are exercises throughout this book that use the tarot cards. Some are more specialized than others, and I will even guide you through finding a significator for each of your chakras and the seven issues they deal with, which you can find listed in the table of contents. You may wish to select a couple of decks just to work with this book, as one deck more than likely won't be enough. This will help ground your healing work and make you more comfortable with integrating the tarot cards into your healing journey. We will be using the tarot as a guide for your healing journey as well as collecting information from each of the seven energy centers by using the seventy-eight cards of the tarot.

Journaling plays a major role in the healing process, and I recommend you dedicate a journal just for the work you do in this book. Your journal will become an extension of this book and will be the place you collect the information you will need for each of the chakras and each of the issues inside the chakras. You will be using your journal for automatic writing, affirmations, problem-solving, and guided writing work. I advise you to not skip or skim over the journal exercises in this book, but instead, sit with all of them, take your time, and be present with the journal work. Allow it, and your relationship developed with the cards, to clear the dialogue pathways to your chakras.

Since this book is a healing journey mapped and guided by the tarot, it's best to work through this book one chakra at a time, starting at the root and moving up, and build energy as you make your way through the exercises, clearing and cleaning each chakra. This will help build a stronger and more flexible chakra core. Work with this book one chapter at a time and allow yourself to be open to the possibility that you might find out something new about yourself. Give yourself permission to release old wounds or shift old outdated beliefs. Most importantly, remember that like all journeys, there is no right or wrong way to reach the destination. Trust yourself to know when to push and when to stop. Listen, feel, and dialogue with the energy as it bubbles up. Take your time and resist the urge to rush. There is no time limit on this work, and the only prize you will receive is one in which you feel healthier, stronger, more confident, and more comfortable with yourself.

## Assessing Your Chakras with a Seven-Card Reversals Spread

In order to begin your tarot healer journey, we first need to take a look at the current state of your seven chakras. For this, we are going to do a seven-card reversals spread. Yes, you read that correctly: all seven of your cards need to be in the reversed position. Over the years, I have found that the most accurate reading of the chakra system is done with upside-down cards. I can only guess why that is, but honestly, I have learned to just accept it and move on. However, my guess is that the chakras move and are not meant to be standing still. Oftentimes upright cards don't leave a lot of room for movement in readings, whereas reversals have moved and aren't the way we expect them to be, which makes them more aligned with moving energy centers. Reversals also allow themselves to be read in a blocked, protected, or retrograding aspect, much the same way chakras tend to be read.

Please don't get too attached to the fact that we will be working with upside-down cards here in the very first exercise. There are no bad cards in this spread, only cards that show us how we might be blocked, where we might need to be more attentive, and what sort of protection we may have wrapped around our energy centers. I have done this exercise with hundreds of clients and students, and they have all been apprehensive about it at first, but the deeper they got into the cards, the more they noticed how magical it was to use the reversed cards.

Like your chakras, we are going to build this spread upward, starting at the root. So go ahead and grab your tarot deck, make sure you have it upside down, and let's start your chakra pillar spread.

Your inner chakra pillar will look something like this:

- *Card 7:* Crown
- *Card 6:* Third Eye
- *Card 5:* Throat
- *Card 4:* Heart
- *Card 3:* Solar Plexus
- *Card 2:* Sacral
- *Card 1:* Root

You don't have to do a deep reading with the cards at this point. Just write down some observations or things that stick out to you. Try not to let your preconceived interpretations take over just yet. Keep your information-gathering intuitive for now. You may want to consider using one of your less used decks, as this may force you to focus more on the images and less on your standard habitual interpretations of the cards themselves. Of course, if what you observe matches up with what you know, then that is fabulous as well. Just don't get too stuck in the mind. Let it flow and play with it. Maybe take note of a repetitive number or suit, and be mindful to see if you have more than two court cards or major arcana cards in the spread, as this might be important later on when we get to the chapter around that particular chakra or chakras. Seeing as we are working with reversed cards here, you may also want to jot down anything that comes up that causes you distress or bums you out when you see a card in a position where you were hoping to see something more positive show up. It may not make sense now, but it might make perfect sense when you get to the chapter surrounding that particular chakra. I also suggest you keep a picture or list of these cards somewhere, as you will be using them in the coming chapters. Keep in mind that this spread is for information only, which we will explore as we move through the book. You see, this book isn't just designed for you to work with each of the chakras in order, building energy, but it is also going to give you one of the biggest chakra tarot readings you have ever had. By the time you have worked your way thought this book, chapter by chapter, section by section, you will have the ultimate tarot card chakra map.

Welcome to the world of the tarot healer.

# 1

# The Root Chakra

In this chapter you are going to explore seven issues the root chakra deals with on a consistent and ongoing basis. These seven issues each have their own section in this chapter, as they all have important information for you regarding the health and well-being of your root chakra. You will also be selecting significator cards for each of these sections. You will need to keep a record of these cards, as you will use them in other parts of this book. I recommend you record everything inside the journal you have selected to be your partner on your journey with this book. This chapter will round out with a tarot healing session for your root chakra, and you will also need the cards you have selected in these sections for the exercise.

The sections are as follows:

1. Foundation

2. Safety

3. Security

4. Stability

5. Connection

6. The Present

7. Material

## Muladhara

The root chakra, or *muladhara*, as it is known in Sanskrit, is the first of the seven primary chakras in your energetic body. It is located at the base of the spine and affects your feet, legs, rectum, descending colon, and skeletal system. It is associated with the color red, and its element is earth. This chakra is the energy center that connects us to our physical body and the world of organic matter and material things. Think of this chakra as a small, glowing red flower at the base of your spine. The healthier it is, the bigger and brighter it blooms, spreading its bright red petals as far and wide as it can. The more the energy slows down inside of it, the darker, harder, and more withered it becomes.

Your root chakra plays a key role in your everyday life and overall survival. Yep, this energy center keeps you alive, and it does so by maintaining a tether to the physical world. The more life-affirming energy that is pumped through that tether, the stronger the root becomes. The root chakra is a pretty important energy center, and its function dictates what sort of energy flows up into the rest of your chakra system. Yet, despite its importance, many people neglect this chakra. Eighty percent of all clients and students I have worked with have had blocked, torn, slow, or toxic root chakras. Talking about the root chakra is kind of like talking to people about fiber; we know it keeps us alive, and we know we should eat more of it to keep our colon functioning properly, but it's just not very sexy. People prefer to talk about other shinier and flashier things, like intuition or protein.

Rising issues in the root chakra is very much a post-modern–world problem because we have become so sedentary. Unlike our ancestors or even our grandparents, we just don't spend as much time outside. It's not overly necessary for our day-to-day existence, thanks to technology and changes in workplace environments. The fact is that regardless of the efforts of the fitness industry, we move the lower parts of our bodies less and less. Most of us sit for long stretches during the day at work and then again during our rest and relaxation time, which means the majority of us don't exercise as much as we really need to. A recent study from the American Cancer Society found a direct link between extended sitting times and death-causing diseases.[1] Do a Google search for "Is sitting killing us?" and just see how many articles pop up. Like it or not, we are squashing our root chakras and not allowing the energy it needs to flow into it and, consequently, into us. Even we writers and tarot readers work our mind and arms more than any other part of our physical body, which is why my step counter is my best friend. The root chakra is the most vulnerable energy center of our entire chakra system, especially as technology continues to make life more convenient.

## EXERCISE
· · · · ·

This first energy center is central to us feeling safe, secure, and stable and feeling connected to, present in, and aligned with the material world. It is the very foundation in which we build our body, mind, and spirit. What happens here in the root chakra affects every other energy center that sits on top of it. Have issues here and you

---

1. Alpa V. Patel, Maret L. Maliniak, Erika Rees-Punia, Charles E. Matthews, and Susan M Gapstur, "Prolonged Leisure Time Spent Sitting in Relation to Cause-Specific Mortality in a Large US Cohort," *American Journal of Epidemiology* 187, no. 10 (October 2018): 2,151–58, https://doi.org/10.1093/aje/kwy125.

are guaranteed to have issues all the way up your chakra system. That is why it is crucial to have an open dialogue with your root chakra. The easiest way to do that is to give it a significator, which is a card that will represent the chakra. I always think about the Emperor and the Queen of Pentacles when I am working with the root chakra, as they both are about building, growing, and supporting, but your significator may be very different.

For this first exercise, grab your tarot deck and place the cards face up. Spread them out and see which image best represents the energy you want to see radiating out of your root chakra. Don't rush selecting this card, as we will be working with it throughout this whole chapter. Take your time and really make sure the card you have selected will stand up to the strain of holding up the rest of your chakra system. Make sure it is strong, stable, and able to hold you in place even in the most difficult of times but also that it is fluid enough to move and flex as you stretch, dance, and grow. Once you have your card, open your journal and do some automatic writing about this card and your root chakra. Do this before you move on to the next section of this chapter, as you may get some interesting information that could deepen your experience as you work through the seven main issues of this chakra.

· · · · ·

## 1. Foundation

The root chakra is the foundation of your chakra system. Think of it this way: it holds up the walls that support the roof to the temple of your body. Nobody wants to build a temple on a rocky, cracked, or shoddy foundation, which is why it always shocks me that so few people pay attention to their energetic foundation. They seem perfectly happy to have it filled with holes, torn at the seams, and crumbling to pieces, and then they wonder why their body doesn't seem to do what they want it to do. Bad foundations create bad buildings and ones that tend to buckle, collapse, and ultimately fall apart. I don't know about you, but I would never build a house to live in on such a disaster of a foundation, nor would I expect something built on fault conditions to hold it together for very long. Imagine having the walls crashing down on you or having the roof cave in on you while you are sleeping. These are nightmare scenarios, yet so many people believe that it is okay to build their body and life this way.

Why do we think allowing this to happen to our root chakra is acceptable?

It is mainly because people believe they can't see it. However, take a look around your health and your life, and you will have plenty of evidence of how strong your foundation is. Your life is either moving along nicely and you feel confident about your growth and the direction you are headed, or you feel blocked, unsure, and shaken at best. Your foundation is evident in every decision you make, every step you take or don't take, and every fear or doubt that whirls around your head. Spend two minutes listening to someone and you will be able to see how strong their foundation is. People speak the conditions of their lives all the time. So be mindful of the words you are using to describe your life, your choices, your circumstances, and your abilities, as they are all either building on your foundation or shattering it. Your body is a mirror of all the decisions you have made at a foundation level, and it is easier than you think to get a picture of what is going on with you at that level.

# EXERCISE

· · · · ·

Grab your journal and your tarot cards, as it's time to dive deeper into your foundation. Shuffle your deck and read over the following questions, pulling a card as your answer.

- *Card 1:* Where does my foundation need assistance?
- *Card 2:* How can I make my foundation stronger?
- *Card 3:* What do I need to do to make sure my foundation is flexible enough not to crack?
- *S:* Root Chakra Significator

Just pull one card for each of these questions, and then spend some time with these cards in your journal. Consider what elements showed up here, as the foundation elements are important. Water could mean you need more flexibility and give in your foundation. The best foundations are the ones with a bit of flow to them. Air could mean you need to cleanse more often, literally blowing away blocks and cobwebs, or it may be showing you where cracks are forming. Fire could mean you need more action and movement in your foundation, and, of course, earth means you need to compact the base and strengthen the foundation. Jot down some key words for each of the cards you pulled and keep them for the next step in this process.

Next, take these three cards and line them up beside your root chakra significator. This will not only give you a lovely four-card spread, but it will also show you in living color what is going on with the foundation energy of your root chakra.

| 1 | 2 | 3 | S |

Grab that list of key words you made in your journal and start forming an intention statement around these four cards. Do your best to focus on the positive aspect of your cards for this exercise. I know it is easy to get lost in the negative meanings of some of the cards, but this is an intention statement, and it needs to have some sort of power, commitment, and motivation behind it. It is hard to do when we are focused on the constricting and heavier energy of the card meanings. I am not asking you to be Pollyanna about it either. I just merely want you to connect with words that have a certain feel to them, words that would move you into growth instead of immobilizing you.

Let me give you an example using the Queen of Pentacles as our significator and the Seven of Swords, the Three of Pentacles, and the Lovers card as the three answer cards. From these four cards, I can create an intention statement like "As I build my foundation, I tap into the grounding and stable energy of the Queen of Pentacles, and I learn to only take on what I need and let the rest go. I know I am stronger and more confident when I am working with others and more flexible when I can love myself for who I am," or "I intend to strengthen my energetic foundation by building on the energy of the queen with collaboration, discernment, and self-care." This intention statement allows you to make a verbal and visual connection to your foundation. It's a simple exercise, but it shifts your focus just enough that you start to become more consciously aware of your energetic foundation, which as we have already discussed, is not the norm. Just by completing this simple exercise, you have already started to repair and restore your root chakra. High five!

Last, it's time to pull a significator for your foundation. This card should represent what your ideal foundational energy is and the energy that you want to build your overall health and well-being upon. Think about the cards in your tarot deck that already have building energy in them: the aces, the pages, and even the fours in the minors; or the Star, Temperance, and even the Hierophant in the majors. All these cards have elements that would make fantastic energetic foundations. Whichever card you select, I want you to go ahead and reverse it. Yep, make it stand on its head, for only in the reversed aspect can you really see if your foundation will hold up. Things look different upside down, so make sure your card works just as well standing on its head as it does on its feet. Take this card, along with the reversed root chakra card you selected in the introduction, to your journal and start creating a dialogue between these two cards. This will give you an even deeper understanding of your body, your life, and the current state of your energetic self.

To end this section, add the reversed card to your collection to give yourself a full six-card spread, which will look something like this:

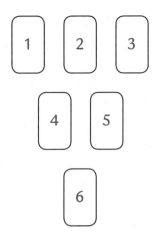

- *Top Row:* Your three journal answer cards from the foundation questions.
- *Middle Row:* Your root chakra significator and foundation significator cards.
- *Bottom Row:* Your reversed root chakra card from your chakra pillar.

This spread is the map to your thoughts, feelings, and beliefs surrounding your foundation. Spend as much time as you can with these cards and gather as much information as possible. Take note of reoccurring themes, numbers, patterns, and elements. These six cards have a powerful story to tell. Allow yourself the space to be open to receive it.

• • • • •

## 2. Safety

The fight-or-flight survival trigger sits here in the root chakra, so it stands to reason that if you are ever in a situation where you don't feel safe, your need for survival will kick in. Survival is about keeping you alive and not much more. It allows you to find a way to see another day. It does not mean that day will be happy, abundant, or filled with joy. You will just live to see it. I point this out not to be a downer, but to show just what safety is. We have a lot of illusions that dwell in the root chakra, and safety is one of them. We like to think we know what it is, what it will feel like, and what sort of experience it will bring. But the truth is most of us are never very truthful about what safety is. We have nice delusions about it being a pile of soft, comfy cushions or a wraparound blanket and a hot beverage that we cradle between our hands, as if this is the most protective bubble in the world. This may make you feel safe, but it isn't what safety is. Being safe is about being alive, and that's your root chakra's programming, basic and primal. This part of your root chakra is always on the look-out for threats, and I do mean always, so unless your life is under an imminent threat, chances are you are pretty safe right now. Even if you have anxiety, even if you aren't happy with your life, you are still safe.

The root chakra can go into hyperdrive when your survival instincts are triggered. It can work overtime and drain energy from the chakras above in order to keep up with the adrenaline coursing through your body. This in turn can cause problems with the adrenals, even though they are not directly connected to your root chakra, which is why once you have calmed down and feel like the threat is over, you will be exhausted. Having these triggers on a constant basis does terrible damage to your body and eventually will weaken your immune system. Overactive chakras are just as damaging to your physical, mental, and spiritual bodies as underactive ones. The safety issue in the root is on the rise, as we see more and more people suffering from panic attacks and anxiety disorders. They honestly believe they are under attack; they don't feel safe, and they feel the world is out to get them. This is a very serious issue and one that should not be taken lightly. I have many clients who suffer from panic attacks, and root chakra work is the only work we do until we can get those attacks under some sort of control. We do this work alongside their medical doctors and oftentimes their therapist.

## EXERCISE
· · · · ·

Let's go ahead and select a card as your safety significator. This is a card that you feel represents your ideal safety situation. It might represent how it looks or how it feels or even how you might think about it. This card builds on your foundation and represents the next step in your root chakra energy. Some suggested cards are the Ace of Pentacles, the King of Swords, the Queen of Cups, the Empress, or even the Sun. This card must align with how you see safety in your life and, unlike in the foundation section, we are going to keep this card in its upright position. Before you pull this card, just take a moment and hold the deck in your hands. Visualize yourself safe, protected, and sitting inside the beautiful red flower. Know that your root chakra is providing all the loving energy you require to maintain this feeling of safety, as you go ahead and find your safety significator. Once you finish your visualization, fan the cards out in front of you face up and select your safety significator.

Take the card to your journal and write why you selected this particular card. What is it about this card that makes you think or feel safe? Once you have written all you can and you have consulted your favorite tarot books, write an affirmation statement or power mantra for this card. I sometimes like to start this process by finding quotes or passages from books on my chosen topic that I like. For this, it would be around safety. As you write your affirmation statement or power mantra, remember you will be placing it somewhere you can see it on a regular basis.

Here are a couple of examples to get you started:

- *I feel safe in the presence of the King of Swords.*
- *The Ace of Pentacles asks me to always look for reminders that I am safe, protected, and taken care of.*
- *The Queen of Cups steadies my emotions so I can feel safe even when the waves of my life feel choppy.*

Your affirmation or power mantra will become a wonderful healing and restoring tool for your root chakra. If you feel inclined to write more than one affirmation or mantra, by all means do so. Just know that one is enough. Once your statement is finished, find somewhere to put it that will allow you to see it, maybe beside your decks, on your altar, or even on your desk.

Let's take this significator card and see how it affects the rest of your chakra energy. Safety is a pretty important energy to be pumping through your body. How safe you feel has tremendous impact on the higher chakras, so let's use your safety significator card and build a safety chakra pillar. For this spread you will pull six additional cards and lay them out like the following diagram, with the root chakra safety significator as card number 1 on the bottom.

- *Card 7:* Crown Chakra
- *Card 6:* Third Eye Chakra
- *Card 5:* Throat Chakra

- *Card 4:* Heart Chakra
- *Card 3:* Solar Plexus Chakra
- *Card 2:* Sacral Chakra
- *Card 1:* Root Chakra Safety Significator

Once you have laid out your cards, see what sort of information they give you. Did you pick a good significator card, and is it having a positive impact on your entire chakra energy? We read these cards as if they are telling us a story, which in this case is how safe we feel inside each of the seven chakras. Each card builds on the next. This means that the cards underneath are always influencing the cards that sit on top of them. This starts with the significator you have sitting at card 1 and how it affects card 2, how card 2 influences card 3, and so on, all the way to the top at card 7. You might find one or two chakra areas have some issues, and I don't want you to freak out if you get cards that don't appear initially to be telling a good story. These cards may have some really important information about how this chakra responds to issues of safety or even how they deal with matters of safety, so be gentle as you deal with cards that might seem scary or off-putting. Just know that there are no bad cards, only lessons to learn, energy to clear, and wounds to still lovingly heal. Take your time moving through the cards in this spread. Sit with each of them in meditation and allow these cards to unfold.

· · · · ·

## 3. Security

I know for some people, security is the same thing as safety, but it isn't. Security is the next level up from survival. Security means you have your basics covered and you don't have to worry about them. Unlike safety, which is always assessing threats to your life, security is about the basic material things you require while you live. This means you have a roof over your head and food in your belly. It means you have the basic requirements for life. If you have ever read the book or watched the film adaptation of *Freakonomics*, you will know that security is obtained pretty early on in our financial journey.[2] You would also be surprised how little money it takes for our security issues to be resolved as a primal root chakra issue, as it is only somewhere between $5,000 and $15,000. Now remember we are only talking the bare minimum to put a roof over your head and food in your stomach, and we are not talking about the quality of that roof or the type and quality of the food. It is important to understand that the root chakra is only triggered when it perceives these things are not being taken care of. So your perception of what security is will be a determining factor of how often and when your root chakra is triggered by this issue. It might be a good idea to flip a card to see what your current perception is. Just do a quick one-card draw and keep this card out, as you will need it later on in this chapter.

In our current world, we have moved away from basic essentials to a laundry list of items we must have or have deemed we need in order to actually feel secure in our lives. Most of the things on that list are nonessential to the primal programming of your root chakra, which means we have, for the most part, tried to reprogram this

---

2. Steven Levitt and Stephen J. Dubner, *Freakonomics* (New York: HarperCollins, 2005).

energy center to keep up with our wants and moved it away from just feeling satisfied by fulfilling needs. This is a problem, as we have now directly linked our security issues to the realm of the ego, which is never satisfied and always feeling undervalued and under attack. In order to get this part of our root chakra functioning, we need to go back to basics. We need to have an honest conversation with ourselves about what is essential in our outer world and what is merely there to appease the ego.

For example, you might have convinced yourself that you won't feel secure until you have $10,000 in savings, you have paid off all your debt, your health is at 100 percent, you have found the partner of your dreams, or fill in the blank. These are all ego needs and have no direct link to security as the root chakra knows it. The absence of the things you claim to need will start to block the flow of energy to your root chakra. You will literally start to slow it down and freeze it with your never-ending list of demands. Slow and sluggish energy centers mean that your body and your mind will feel sluggish and slow as well, which ultimately can turn into some form of depression or ongoing feelings of sadness.

## EXERCISE
· · · · ·

In a world that is striving for happiness, joy, and enlightenment, it might be time to reexamine what we think we want versus what we actually need. Pick up your deck, give it a shuffle, and fan out your cards. Now let's take a closer look at what's going on in your center of security and how it might be affecting the function of your root chakra. For this spread, you are going to pull four cards and place them around your root chakra card from your original spread in the introduction for this book. Your cards will be laid out like the diagram below, and they will represent the following:

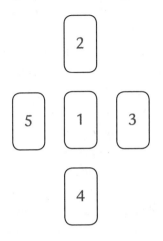

- *Card 1:* Reversed Root Chakra Card
- *Card 2:* Emotional Security
- *Card 3:* Financial Security
- *Card 4:* Mental Security
- *Card 5:* Physical Security

Now that your key security points are mapped out in your spread, what story do they tell, and how do they tie into the root chakra card from your chakra pillar? Things to look for in regard to this spread are the reversed cards, court cards that might show you either how you see yourself or how you need to see yourself, and the major arcana cards, which will give you some idea of bigger concepts at play in your area of security. Journal with these cards for a while, until you feel you have run out of things to say, and then go and find your favorite tarot books and dive deeper.

Let's see if we can pull all the information we have collected thus far together.

Grab the card you flipped at the beginning of this section, the one that shows the current perception of your personal security, and place it next to the reversed root chakra card from the previous spread. Then add your foundation significator card, so you now have three cards in front of you. Go ahead and pick your security significator. This will be different from the card you just randomly flipped, because you will be choosing this card on purpose, deliberately. Turn your cards over, start scanning the images, and select the one that shows the image you want as your symbol of security. Then place it next to the foundation significator. You should now have four cards:

```
┌─────┐  ┌─────┐  ┌─────┐  ┌─────┐
│     │  │     │  │     │  │     │
│  1  │  │  2  │  │  3  │  │  4  │
│     │  │     │  │     │  │     │
└─────┘  └─────┘  └─────┘  └─────┘
```

- *Card 1:* Security Perception
- *Card 2:* Reversed Root Chakra Card
- *Card 3:* Foundation Significator
- *Card 4:* Security Significator

This is a snapshot of all the energy, healing, and clearing swirling around in your root chakra and the energy that wants to expand, grow, or be cleaned out. If there is a massive contrast between the random card, your selected card one, and your security significator card, you will know you have some healing to do. If they are similar, then perhaps there is an underlying message here that needs to be explored at a deeper, more meditative way. I suggest you do some pathworking with these cards, which means to use them to journey with or as part of a visualization. Set them up on an altar space, if you have one, or the top of a bookshelf works nicely as well.

Light a tea light candle, grab your favorite grounding or root chakra stone/crystal, and just focus on your breath work, making sure the breath is being pushed all the way down into the root ball at the base of your spine. As you breathe, gaze into these cards and let them be your only focus. Travel your gaze over each of the four cards slowly, taking in the colors, shapes, and images. Take your time and just allow whatever needs to bubble up to rise within you. Do not hold on to it; instead breathe it out via the root chakra. See the breath pushing it all out of the base of your spine. To add some healing energy to this, you can hold the palms of your hands over your legs and on each exhale, swipe the air above your legs away from your body. Do this until you feel you have cleared what needs to be cleared for now. Trust yourself to know when this exercise feels complete.

When you feel done, complete, and relaxed, end your pathworking with these cards. You can keep the tea light going if you feel inclined to; otherwise, just blow it out. If you have a burning desire to journal about your pathwork journey, by all means do so. The more information you can gather, the more you can heal, restore, and realign your root chakra energy.

· · · · ·

## 4. Stability

I know at this point you are wondering if I have already covered this area, as it seems stability is a lot like security and safety, but the truth is stability is very different. Here we are talking about a core strength, something so fundamental to our being that it's like being tethered to a rock, while we're also allowed to flex and flow like a piece of bamboo. If anything, stability is more about strength, resilience, determination, and grit. It is in the area of stability that we build on the issues that came before it. We have laid our foundation, we have made sure we are safe, we have examined any potential risks to our life, and now we are ready to dig in and ground our root chakra energy deep into our core. It is virtually impossible to have stability in one's life if the above issues are not taken care of first. The differences in the issues inside the root chakra may seem subtle, but they are significant and substantial.

You may think you have figured out your foundation, and maybe even feel pretty good about your current level of safety and security. But what if you suddenly got ill or you lost your job? How stable would your life feel then? The truth is most of us don't do well when life throws us curveballs. We all tend to falter at times, and it is human to do so. Stability is an illusion, and it only takes the slightest tilt to our lives to show us just how much of an illusion it really is. Think about the last time you felt like the carpet of your life got pulled out from under your feet, and now see if you can remember how you felt about it. Did it feel like you were untethered and out of control? Did you automatically allow the ego to put you into the role of the victim, or were you able to feel the unsettling energy but not allow it to push you off your course?

You see, that is really what stability is. It allows us to keep moving forward, regardless of the conditions around us or the circumstances that cross our path along the way of life. This doesn't mean you won't have times in your life when you fall apart or have a Tower moment, or when you give yourself a moment to have a small, but much needed, pity party, as seen in the Five of Cups—it just means you won't linger there. If your core stability is functioning, you can allow yourself to feel your moment-to-moment energy and any hurt or pain that arises, but you will not allow it to impact who you are, where you are going, or what you are doing. In fact, when your inner stability is resilient, you may actually find joy in your Tower moments, as you will see them as a necessary part of your growth and expansion.

## EXERCISE
· · · ·

What do you want your inner core to look or feel like?

Think about how it may need to bend, move, or flex under some of life's more testing moments. Also, consider how you want this to be an extension of the other energy you are building inside the root chakra. Some cards to consider might be the Ten of Cups, Ten of Pentacles, the Ace of Wands, and, of course, the Strength card. Once you have selected your card, make sure it is in the reversed aspect. Yes, I want you to keep this card upside down, just like we did in the foundation section. Putting this card on its head will not diminish its ability to be stable. If anything, it should be able to show you that it is just as strong on its head as it is on its feet. Keep this card out, as we are going to use it for our stability spread.

For the stability spread, you are going to remove the major arcana from your deck and separate the suits of the minor arcana into piles. Pick up your suit of cups and give them a shuffle. Fan the cards out face down and select just one card. This card represents your level of emotional stability at this present moment and how well you deal with situations that arise from an emotional point of view. Once you have your card, put the cups away and pick up the swords. Repeat the steps and select your card. This card represents your current mental state, meaning how well you can focus, clear your mind, and stay on task, regardless of what is going on around you. Put the swords away, pick up the suit of wands, and repeat the steps to select your card. This card represents your level of spiritual faith. Do you believe the universe/God is working with you or against you? Now, put the wands away and select your final card from the suit of pentacles. This card represents how stable you think your material world is. Do you control your world, or does your world control you?

- *Card 1:* Stability Significator
- *Card 2:* Emotional Stability
- *Card 3:* Mental Stability
- *Card 4:* Spiritual Stability
- *Card 5:* Material Stability

Look closely at these cards now that you have them lined up in a nice neat column. How is your concept of stability? Do you feel good about what you see, or does it surprise you? Keep in mind that this is just a snapshot of what energy is currently swirling around in your root chakra, but it is not a permanent energy, nor is it one that cannot be changed, adjusted, or realigned. If you have some painful or uncomfortable cards, know that these are things you can explore during your meditation and energy work. You might even consider aligning these cards with a pocket crystal, as a reminder that these concerns are still areas of healing and clearing for you. Take this spread to your journal and explore the cards more deeply. Really dig into the card meanings and read some additional tarot books to get even more insight. Keep your writing and research focused on the area of stability so you don't get lost going down irrelevant rabbit holes of information.

Once you have finished your journal work, consider placing your painful or uncomfortable cards on your altar, along with any crystals or pocket stones you may have aligned with them, and light a candle as you visualize your root chakra flower blooming underneath you. Breathe in the images on the cards and the hurt or concerning feelings they bring with them, and then on the exhale, push those feelings out. Imagine them leaving your body with each exhale, pushing them out with your breath on purpose and with healing intent. When you feel you have pushed out all you can, breathe deeply and let the root chakra flower send loving energy up through your root ball at the base of your spine, all the way up your back and out the top of your head. Smile as you feel this safe and stable energy move up and down your spine, making you feel strong, confident, and resilient.

When you are done with your visualization, put your cards back into your deck and blow out your candle. If you did align the cards with pocket stones, place them in your pocket and know that they have been infused with stability energy. You are now ready to move on to the next section.

· · · · ·

## 5. Connection

You may have heard yourself or someone you know say the words "I felt deeply connected" or maybe "I feel so disconnected." This, dear tarot healer, is root chakra language. How connected or disconnected we feel to people, places, and experiences depends on how connected we feel to our bodies and the world at large. Happy, joyful, and engaged people tend to have a sense of connection, either to their purpose, their community, or their immediate families. This connection comes from a deep connection to themselves, who they are, and why they are here. People who feel disconnected, however, tend to constantly feel lost, out of sorts, misplaced, or even forgotten. These people do not feel connected to their surroundings and oftentimes don't feel very comfortable in their own skins. More than likely you have experienced both of those feelings at some point in your life. I know I certainly have. In fact, I would say I have more often felt uncomfortable in my skin than comfortable in it. For me, getting older has helped, as with each passing year I feel more and more aligned to my sense of self and my connection to the world at large. Therefore, hang in there. It does get better, and sometimes we just don't hit our stride until later in life.

We are all born with this need for connection. As babies, we are programmed to bond with maternal figures for our own sense of survival. We need to feel contact, love, and support from the moment we come screaming into the world. This is one of our primal core needs, but we don't all get it, which can cause major damage very early on to the root chakra. It isn't anything that can't be repaired, but it does take consistent effort and a commitment to see it through until the job is done. This sense of connection is not just an important human need, but it is more than likely the most spiritual need we have as well. Ever since we evolved into the humanoid forms we are now, we have sought out something bigger, such as a god, goddess, or divine power that made us and is connected to us in some form. Therefore, it is no coincidence that we have two connection points in our energetic body, the one in the root and the one in the crown chakra. In many respects, our need for connection is part of our desire to belong, and some of us aren't overly picky about where we find that sense of belonging.

Like most of the issues in the root chakra, this connection, or need to belong, is not one that can happen outside of ourselves. However, a lot of people who feel disconnected seek this feeling, this primal core need, in things outside of who they are. Many seek it in religion, sex, and drugs, among other things. The connection point in the root chakra is all about feeling like this physical existence has a point. There is a reason you are in your current body and that you are having the physical experiences you are having. Your body is connected to this physical plane for a reason. The stronger our sense of connection, the more deeply connected we are to the physical world. In energy work, we call this grounding. Keeping ourselves grounded and anchored to the physical plane is what this point of connection does in the root. It is something we feel, not something we find.

So how is your point of connection, and are you grounded into your body and the physical plane?

## EXERCISE
· · · · ·

Grab a tarot deck, give it a shuffle, and just hold it for a few seconds, as we prepare to choose a significator card for your root chakra point of connection. Close your eyes, take a nice, deep breath, and focus on the word *connection*. See each individual letter appear on the screen of your mind like you are magically typing it into your brain. Once you can see the whole word clearly, fan out your cards face down and pick just one. Now make sure this card is reversed, so if you selected an upright card, flip it. If you drew the card reversed, keep it that way, as we are going to work with this card in the protection aspect. This card is showing you your current state of connection and disconnection, with a focus on both. Seeing as we are focusing on this card in the protection aspect, what part of you is it protecting? Did you get water/emotions, earth/health, air/thoughts, or fire/faith? Or perhaps you selected a major arcana card, so the lesson is more profound.

Take a moment to really look at the card, in its upside-down form as well, and notice what is now at the top of the card that used to be at the bottom. It is important, and one of the reasons we flip cards, to see what we might have overlooked. What is now at the top of your card is what you have not been seeing, a point in your connection hose that has had a kink in it and now needs your attention to help straighten it out and get things flowing and moving again.

Grab your journal and start writing about this card and how you see it in relation to connection and disconnection. I recommend you create two columns on a blank piece of paper and label one column *connection* and the other *disconnection*. Fill these columns with key words from your card, starting intuitively and with what you can see. Maybe just having the card reversed creates a sense of disconnection for you, and if this is the case, write "The figure is upside down with their feet in the air" in your disconnection column. When you can't come up with other words for your lists, pick up your favorite tarot books and explore this card, seeking out words similar to *connection* and *disconnection*. This list of key words will be helpful when you are moving into doing some energy work with this issue. When you feel you have written all you can, pick your deck back up and give it another shuffle, leaving the card you just selected out and in front of you. Pull a card to answer each of the following questions:

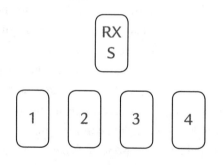

- *RX S:* Reversed Significator
- *Card 1:* What action can I take to feel more connected to my body?
- *Card 2:* What action can I take to feel more connected to my home?
- *Card 3:* What action can I take to feel more connected to my community?
- *Card 4:* When I am feeling disconnected, what action can I take to restore my sense of belonging?

These four cards, which will be in their upright position, in addition to the first card you pulled, will give you a more complete picture of how the energy of connection and disconnection are currently working in your root chakra. Continue to keep in mind that this can and does change, but you have five cards with a lot of information in them. Work with them slowly, and don't rush it. Practice sitting with each card in meditation, visualizing the card inside your root chakra surrounded by red light and growing roots, roots that will sprawl out and make connections of their own. See your key words in these roots as they spread out and travel more deeply into the earth, securing you firmly into the physical plane. Let the energy of the earth flow back up through those roots and energize your body. Feel it move up your spine, making you feel strong, stable, and connected.

Once you have finished meditating with these cards, go back to your journal and see if anything you wrote about your significator card has changed. If not, that is perfectly fine. It just means you might need to do the exercise more than once to see or feel a shift. If it has, write about how and why you think that is before moving on to the next section of this chapter.

• • • • •

## 6. The Present

The root chakra deals with the right now—not the past, not the future, but the moment you are in. When we think about all the issues this chakra deals with, it is only logical that it can't see behind the energy that now surrounds it. This is one of the keys to healing and restoring this energy center, because you can change how you think, feel, act, or react in this moment. You can ask yourself if you are safe, if you are secure, if you feel stable and connected right now, this second, while you take a breath. Understanding that the root chakra doesn't deal in the past and can't see beyond the moment is a liberating and important lesson. When we remind ourselves that being in the moment benefits the root chakra, we also remind ourselves that being in the moment helps us feel safe, helps us make a connection with our bodies and the world that surrounds us, and makes us able to move forward and grow.

Being present, however, seems to be harder to do now than it ever was before. We live in a world of distractions. We are constantly being asked to answer for the past and make plans for the future. No matter where we turn, someone or something is trying to move us out of the moment we stand in. How many times have you driven to a destination and not really remembered how you got there or lost track of the time it took? Somewhere during the journey, you lost your connection with the present moment and allowed your focus to drift away, either off to the future or to the past or maybe off to a totally different reality. Driving a car is one of those times when our lives and the lives of others depend on us being present, grounded, and rooted to our task. Yet the reality is many of us are not, and we have all had moments where we have had to remind ourselves to stay focused on the road and all that entails.

At this point, those of you familiar with chakra work might be trying to convince yourself that this is not a root chakra issue but a higher chakra concern, and that maybe this present-moment stuff is all about awareness and we should not be talking about this until we get to the third eye or crown chakra. This is a common mistake and one of the reasons a lot of people struggle with opening up their third eye, connecting to their intuition and allowing themselves to truly expand and grow their awakened awareness. If you can't get it right here at the root, you won't be able to get it further up the chakra pillar. Here, in the root, is where it all begins and from where the energy grows. It is from the root we draw up the energy we wish to expand and grow, but it must be here first. You can't grow a seed that doesn't exist. Go on, try—I dare you.

## EXERCISE
· · · · ·

The aces in the tarot are often referred to as seed cards, and they make perfect significators for the present-moment energy needed in the root chakra. Each of the aces gives us a moment of awareness. They remind us that in every movement we are dealing with something material, something emotional, something spiritual, and something mental. The aces also show us possibilities, things that have not yet happened but might possibly happen someday, if you know how to grow your seed. The present moment is the same. It shows us what is possible, not what could be (because that's in the future) and not what was (because that is in the past), but what might grow if we can place our focus and attention on it in the moment.

Let's explore this further by removing the four aces from your deck and laying them out face up in front of you. One of these cards is your significator for the present energy in your root chakra. Maybe you instinctively know what seed you want to grow, and if that is the case, just select your card now and put the other three cards away. If, however, you have no idea what seed you need right now, take a nice, deep breath and place your hand on your heart. Ask this question out loud: "What seed needs to be planted into my root chakra today?" Now place the same hand over the four cards in front of you and see which one gives off a response. It may be tingling in your fingers, with heat in your palm or even coldness. One of these four cards is responding to your question, so open yourself to it and allow it to answer, even if it is a quiet, timid response.

Once you have your significator, it is time to take it to your journal and explore this possibility further. Think of this card as a proposition from the universe, as if it is telling you, "Here is what I am offering, if you are willing to do the work." As you journal with this card, imagine yourself saying yes to this offer, and see if you can visualize the action steps you would take once you have agreed to grow this seed. Write about how you will prepare the ground for this seed and what sort of feeding and watering regime this seed will require. Remember not to allow yourself to get caught up in the future aspects of this seed, and stay focused on what happens now, once you have accepted it, and what it means for your time, your energy, your health, and even your bank account. This card is only the offer; it is not the end result. When you have written all you can intuitively, grab your favorite tarot books and see if you can gather any other information that is relevant to your seed and the present moment. Then, close this section out by simply closing your eyes and seeing yourself plant your seed deep into the earth.

Congratulations! You have just planted something in the present moment that will benefit your future self for years to come.

· · · · ·

## 7. Material

As a Gen Xer, I grew up with songs by Madonna, and all the girls I grew up with knew we were material girls. If you have no idea what I am talking about, go to YouTube and type in "Material Girl by Madonna." Yes, it's corny and hasn't aged well, but make it your theme song for this section anyway, as your root chakra will love you for it. Whether you like to admit it or not, we do live in a material world, which is made of matter and is full of things, including us. The biggest mistake people make here in the root chakra is thinking that this energy center has feelings, because it doesn't, nor does it deal with morals or ethics. It is a base, primal, survival chakra. Its only job is to cover your basic life needs, and material things are a part of that. The root chakra also doesn't deal in guilt or shame, which are feelings people wrap around their material things. We will explore this more in the next chapter, in the sections on desire and pleasure. But for the sake of the root chakra, let's keep it simple and basic, because that's all you have down here anyway.

You need food, water, and shelter. These things are not free, at least not in the majority of the world, which means we need a way to pay for them. This is about the time money creeps into the root chakra and says hello. Money is our current currency, and it is how we pay for our basic survival needs. You might be able to barter for some of them, but not all. Money makes the world turn. We don't have to like it, and we don't even have to enjoy being a part of it, but we do have to accept the fact that money is a requirement of the root chakra in our current timeline. Although we don't always need money to obtain things, money will have played a part in the creation of those things at some point, which means when we deal with any issues concerning the material world, we are going to have to deal with money issues. This is why Madonna knew she had to become a material girl. I know this example is corny, but it will stick in your mind.

## EXERCISE

· · · · ·

Our relationship with money will have an impact on the health and well-being of our root chakra, which in turn will eventually impact the health and well-being of our body. Health and money are related, as you will see in the suit of pentacles. The suit of pentacles deals almost exclusively with the material aspect of our physical lives. The pentacles show how we use our five senses and how we navigate the world of things. Sometimes this suit is all about the money, hence why it can be known as the suit of coins. At other times, the traditional form of pentacles represents a mix of health, overall well-being, and the complicated relationship we have with the material world. For this exercise, we are only going to use the suit of pentacles, so remove this suit from your deck and put the other cards away.

First, we are going to intuitively draw a significator for this issue inside your root chakra. Shuffle your pentacles and fan them out in front of you face down. Place your hand on your heart and take a few nice, deep breaths and ask the following question out loud: "How am I engaging in my relationship with the world of material things?" Take your hand from your heart and move it gently over the cards lying face down in front of you until one of these cards answers you. It might be a tingle, a flash of heat, or even a cold chill. Just be open to the answer. Once you have your card, turn it over.

If you selected one of the court cards, this card is letting you know what stage your relationship is in. If you picked the page, then you are at the beginning stages. The knight means you are still learning how to work together. The queen means you are finding your strengths and learning how to negotiate the terms of the relationship so it is balanced and fair, and the king means you have a good understanding of your role inside this complex relationship.

If you selected one of the numbered cards, however, you will have a clear message on what energy is surrounding your relationship with the material world. If you have the ace, chances are you see the world full of possibilities just waiting to be explored. The two might show you how you feel you are always juggling and trying to make ends meet, while the three shows you know we are all in this together, and we have a very unique part to play in our material world. The four reminds us that it is easy to feel there is not enough to go around and we need to hold on to whatever we can, whereas the five show us the consequences of cutting ourselves off from others and trying to go it alone. The Six of Pentacles shows an understanding that the material world has a flow to it, and that what goes out comes back in, while the seven shows that everyone gets a harvest season, even you. Eight is all about the hard work, meaning the material world may offer opportunities, but you believe you have to work hard for them and to keep them showing up. The Nine of Pentacles has a feeling of safety and security to it, showing us all that the material world offers if we don't get too caught up in it, and finally the

Ten of Pentacles reminds us that there is always enough to go around and that when we understand we are all in this together, we all have enough.

How is your relationship?

Does it need work, or are you in a good place with your material self?

Take your significator card to your journal and explore it further, first intuitively, and then dive deeper with your favorite tarot books. If you got any of the cards that seem constricted and tight, like the Two, Four, and Five of Pentacles, explore what would happen if you let this belief and its energy go from inside of your root chakra. Write about how liberating yourself from this contracted position will make your body feel. Regardless of what card you drew today, know that it won't stay that way, so do not be discouraged, especially if you got a card that made you feel uncomfortable. Nothing is forever—not you, not me, and not the card you just flipped over. Just understand that it has relevance for right now and is presenting itself for healing, because this is a healing book and you are reading it— which, by the way, is very brave. Once you have finished your journal work with this card, put it together with all the other significator cards you have drawn in this section, as you are going to need them for the tarot healing coming up next.

· · · · ·

## Root Chakra Tarot Healing

Now that you have worked through the seven key issues of the first chakra, it is time to do some energy healing work on all that you have discovered, all that has bubbled up, and all that has presented itself for cleaning and clearing. Grab your tarot deck and get out the significator cards for the issues covered in this chapter. Select your significator card for the root chakra and place it in front of you. This card is going to be the middle card in your root chakra wheel.

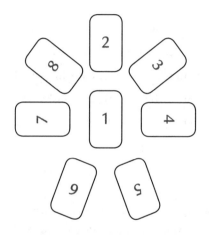

Your card order is as follows:

- *Card 1:* Root Chakra Significator
- *Card 2:* Foundation Significator
- *Card 3:* Safety Significator
- *Card 4:* Security Significator
- *Card 5:* Stability Significator
- *Card 6:* Connection Significator
- *Card 7:* Present Significator
- *Card 8:* Material Significator

Your center card is going to be the energy you will see flowing in and out of the other cards, as if a beautiful red smoke wisps out of the card and starts to tickle the other cards around it. As we move into the visualization part of this exercise, move your hands over the cards as you say the following affirmations for each of the cards surrounding your root chakra significator. The tarot mandala helps anchor your energy healing work and allows you to engage more fully with the overall process. Your affirmations are as follows:

- *Card 2:* I am solid in my foundation.
- *Card 3:* I am safe in all parts of my life.
- *Card 4:* I am secure in who I am and why I am here.
- *Card 5:* I am stable, strong, and unshakable.
- *Card 6:* I am connected deeply to the physical world.
- *Card 7:* I am allowing myself to be present.
- *Card 8:* I am a material being in a material world.

Find somewhere comfortable and quiet, where you won't be disturbed for up to twenty minutes. Place your cards where you can see them and start rubbing your palms gently together as you focus on your breathing. Rub your hands together for about forty seconds, activating the energy centers in your palms. You might start to feel some heat in your hands, and this is good. Now place your hands above your knees and focus on your breath, inhaling through your nose. Feel the breath as it hits the back of your throat, fills your lungs, and expands your belly. As you exhale from the mouth, feel the breath leaving your body and notice the depression of the abdomen. Let the breath work become automatic, and shift your focus to your cards, starting with the center card, which is your root chakra significator. Visualize the red smoke gently rising from the card and twirling around the wheel you have created around it. Each time you exhale, the smoky wisps extend farther and farther. Sit like this for a few minutes, just doing the breath work and keeping your hands on your knees as you feel your chest rise and fall, and visualize the smoky red energy infusing your spread.

When you feel ready, move your hands to your tarot mandala and move them along each card as you speak the corresponding affirmation statements out loud. Read through the entire list three times. Once you have finished, just relax and focus on the breath work, placing your hands back on your knees. As you inhale, feel the smoky red energy coming into your nose, hitting the back of your throat, filling up your lungs, and moving into the base of your spine infusing the root chakra. Relax into this, as you inhale all this lovely infused energy, and let this energy clean and clear your root chakra as it embeds your affirmations into your chakra. When this feels complete, remove your hands and just breathe normally for thirty to forty seconds. Thank your cards, and you are done.

You can repeat this simple tarot healing session anytime you want, and by all means, journal about how the session made you feel or any revelations you had during the session. The more you know, the more you inquire, the more you heal.

# 2

# The Sacral Chakra

Inside this chapter you are going to explore seven issues the sacral chakra deals with on a consistent and ongoing basis. These seven issues each have their own section in this chapter, as they all have important information for you regarding the health and well-being of your sacral chakra. You will also be selecting significator cards for each of these sections as you did in the previous chapter. This chapter will round out with a tarot healing session for your sacral chakra, for which you will need the cards you have selected as significators in the sections in this chapter.

The sections are as follows:

1. Creativity

2. Birth and Rebirth

3. Grief

4. Desire

5. Memory

6. Pleasure

7. The Past

## Svadhishthana

The sacral chakra, or *svadhishthana,* as it is known in Sanskrit, is the second chakra. It is located in the pelvic area, and it affects your reproductive system, hips, bladder, kidneys, and your entire lymphatic system. Energetically speaking, this is where your emotions reside, which makes the second chakra the control center for your emotional body. It also governs your body's water and the many waterways flowing under your skin. Needless to say, a large majority of people have profound and deep issues in this chakra, because very few humans have any sort of mastery over their emotions. I know I don't, and I've been working on my emotional body for over a decade. If we were all nice, emotionally stable people, authors like Brené Brown and Anne Lamott and the entire spiritual and self-help industries would be out of business. Generally speaking, humans are horrible with emotions, even though we are emotional beings. Everything about being human is an emotional experience, which makes what we learn here in this chakra so vitally important. Yet, just like the root chakra, so many skip this chakra and are in too much of a hurry to get to the top of the chakra pillar. But not you, right? You know you have to work slowly, build your inner energy, gain resilience, find your grit, and take it one chakra at a time.

I'm not going to sugarcoat it. We deal with some pretty deep, dark crap here in the second chakra, for it is not only where life begins but also where it ends. We deal with both death and birth in this chakra, not to mention all the emotions that each of these trigger. It is here in the second chakra that we decide what stays with us, what gets pushed up into the next chakra, and what we delegate to our shadow side. The *shadow* was a term first coined by Carl Jung to explain the parts of ourselves we reject or disassociate with. These are the parts of who we are that we like to deny and feel do not align with the core of who we say we are. This is not to say that we only put negative traits in our shadow vault. On the contrary, we also put positive traits there and parts of ourselves that could actually make our lives better. It may seem unbelievable that we would do such a thing, but we do. We never allow any part of ourselves that does not align with what we believe our self-image to be to come out of the shadow, and all of this gets decided upon right here, in the second chakra. As I said, deep stuff.

I totally understand why people want to avoid this chakra, as there is nothing light and fluffy about it. We have to face some pretty hard issues here. Just be warned that if you have spent a good part of your life pushing away the dark side of yourself or if you didn't want to see hard truths being reflected back to you by your sacral chakra waters, you will possibly struggle with this chakra. It is in this chakra we first learn to be kind to ourselves as well, which will be helpful since, to put it in second-chakra terms, there are times when doing the work with this chakra that you might find yourself drowning. It can be tough here in the second chakra, and we need to be able to show ourselves just as much nurturing energy as we would other people. The choppy emotional waters of the second chakra need to be learned, and you can't control them, so don't even bother. However, you will learn to ride them and navigate them. Just know you might get smashed on the rocks of your memories and swept away by the powerful undercurrent of your emotions.

## EXERCISE
· · · · ·

Before you strap on your flippers and snap your googles into place so that you can dive into this chapter, you need to find a significator for your second chakra. You are going to choose this card strategically, and by this, I mean you are going to have your cards out in front of you, face up, and deliberately select your significator. This card needs to have a hint of strength, a dash of flexibility, a good dose of flow, and the ability to stand on its head while underwater. Yes, your card needs to be upside down. Recommended cards are Temperance, the Star, the Moon, Judgement, the Queen and King of Cups, the Two of Wands, and the Six of Swords.

Once you have selected your card, take a moment to connect it to your second chakra. To do this, place the card in your line of sight, upside down of course. Place one hand over your lower pelvis area, as this is where your second chakra sits, and take a couple of nice, deep breaths. Imagine an orange light coming out between your fingers and wrapping around your card. Stay like this for two to three minutes, and then just shake your hands out as you take another nice, deep breath. Next, do some automatic writing in your journal about your upside-down card. Just write whatever pops into your head and, like your second chakra, let it flow. Don't try to control it, don't try and make sense of it, just go with it. When you have run out of inspired words to spill onto the page, pick up your favorite tarot books and dig a little deeper into the card that will, for the rest of this book at least, be your major second chakra influence. Once you are done writing, it's time to dive in, slide in, or perhaps just dip your big toe into the waters of your second chakra. Come on, be brave. I am right here holding a life preserver, and I won't let you drown, I promise.

· · · · ·

# 1. Creativity

We are all, every single one of us, creative. Creative energy is interwoven into every human, without exception. The issue is that most people have very limited ideas about what creativity is. First of all, creativity is not artistic, though art and art forms are one form of creativity. However, they are not the only way to engage in creative energy, and it is this confusion that has closed people off from exploring their creative potential. People tell me all the time they are not creative, but what they are really saying is that they are not artistic, and it is not the same thing. Steven Jobs once said, "Creativity is just connecting things."[3] It's just a way to connect one thing to another, which makes creativity a form of problem-solving. You might be creative with numbers like an accountant, you might be creative with contracts like a lawyer, or you might be creative with strategy like a gamer. There are literally thousands of ways to be creative, and being artistic is just one of them. Therefore, stop saying you are not a creative person, because you are, and denying this part of yourself is not only damaging your second chakra, but it is causing problems in the chakras above this one as well.

When we are not harnessing our creative energy in the second chakra, we stunt our ability to express ourselves in the third chakra, which in turn causes frustration and makes us feel like we are not being heard in the fifth chakra, which can then shut off our intuitive senses in the sixth chakra, and make us close our connection to the divine self in the seventh chakra. In other words, settling here in the second chakra sets you up for mediocre and unfulfilled experiences further up the chakra pillar. To be honest, this is one of the reasons I love tarot so much, because for me it is a form of creative energy. It allows us to

---

3. Steve Jobs, "Steve Jobs: The Next Insanely Great Thing," interview by Gary Wolf, *Wired*, February 1, 1996, https://www.wired.com/1996/02/jobs-2/.

explore information in a very creative way. Whether you like to dive deeper into the numbers, the elements, the astrology, the Kabbalah, or the deeper Christian religious elements on the cards, or even the way the cards themselves create patterns, there is something very creative about using them. How we use, read, store, spread, shuffle, and select our cards is a second-chakra process. Yes, I know, you thought it was a sixth-chakra issue, which is a common mistake. However, we are not talking about intuition here, although it feels similar, but instead we are talking about tapping into creative energy. Your actions with your cards are dictated first by the second chakra, then the fourth, then the fifth, then the sixth, then the seventh, then the third, and down to the first. We use the cards to problem-solve and to give us answers and insights into areas of our lives that perhaps we can't see or don't want to see. This is creative energy.

Let's get creative and select a card, shall we?

## EXERCISE
· · · · ·

It's time to select a significator for your creative energy. This time around you are going to select a card from the court cards and only the court cards. The reason for this is you want to see yourself as a creative person, not an artistic one. You want to be able to see yourself as a cocreator with the universe, playing your part in the larger creative web of humanity, connecting dots, and getting things done in ways that are unique to you. Go ahead and remove your court cards from your deck and place them in front of you face up. Pages represent childlike energy because they use their sense of wonder to be creative. The pages think less about what they can't do, and instead they strive to try as many things as possible. Knights are explorers and seekers, like routine, and will often use creativity to form new habits, achieve new personal goals, and go on as many adventures as possible. Kings and queens have a level of expertise, and they harness their creative energy for very specific reasons. They always have an end in mind, which drives their creative fires. You could say at this level, creativity is linked to desire. They want something, and they will connect as many dots as necessary to get it.

The suits will let you know how your creative energy presents itself. Cups (water) tend to show up in people who are physically moved by their creative process, and they feel the creative energy in them and move through their bodies. Wands (fire) tend to show up in people who often find themselves fired up with sudden bursts of inspiration. This sort of creative energy tends to come and go quickly. Swords (air) show a very cerebral, creative process through thinking, analyzing, and sorting information inside one's mind, whereas pentacles (earth) are a tactile form of creative energy and tend to show for people who like to have all five of their senses involved in the creative process.

Which one are you?

If you don't intuitively and instinctually know which of these cards you are, flip them over so you can't see them. Shuffle them around a bit, and then scan your hand over the tops of the sixteen cards. Just hold the question "Who am I as a creative being?" in your mind as you scan the cards. Once you notice a response from the cards, be it heat, coldness, or a tingle in your fingertips, select your card. If you selected a page, it means you are at your most creative during play. If you selected a knight, you are most creative when you have a routine. If you selected a queen, your creativity comes alive when you are networking and socializing, as you need to be in a group flow situation. If you selected a king, you are your most creative when you are planning, building, and conquering your goals. Next, journal with your card and think about how the person in this card acts and how they may, or may not, problem-solve. Knowing how you engage with your creative energy is important, and this significator card just gave you the key to open that creative door even further.

. . . . .

## 2. Birth and Rebirth

For those of you already familiar with the chakras, I am sure hearing that birth is an essential part of the second chakra isn't a new idea for you. For those of you new to this whole chakra business, remember that both the male and the female genitals are surrounded by the sacral chakra, meaning all our reproductive organs are in this chakra's domain. However, the idea of death and rebirth in the second chakra is not so widely taught. Stillbirth, miscarriage, sterility, and menstruation all happen in the second chakra, literally. The second chakra is where we learn that death and birth are one and the same, which is why we tend to talk about the concept of rebirth in regard to the second chakra. Rebirth is the cycle of life and death. It is the continuous creative energy that happens in the second chakra, and oftentimes this can be traumatic, because in order for something to be born, something must die. Rebirth is both simultaneous and cyclic. It can happen in the moment or over time. It is probably one of the most difficult issues to deal with in this chakra, and that's saying something, considering what else lives here.

Generally speaking, Westerners aren't that great with death and letting go. We tend to wrap a lot of guilt and shame around walking away from things, setting boundaries, saying no, and waving goodbye. Admitting something is over, done, or dead is just not something most people are comfortable with, which is why some people continue to water dead plants, take forever to throw out dead flowers, and leave holiday decorations up long past the holiday season. Hoarding is a growing first-world problem. I think the popularity of the TV show *Hoarders* and the success of Marie Kondo's book *The Life-Changing Magic of Tidying Up* are proof that we might have issues with this second chakra issue of rebirthing.

Like it or not, in order to bring life into the world, be it physical or creatively metaphorical, something needs to die, a cycle needs to end, and you have to say goodbye to something. Birthing a new baby kills the cycle of pregnancy, and you have to say goodbye to sleep and the life you knew before this constant eating and pooping machine took over your life. If you are starting or birthing a new job, your old job and everything that was tied to it dies. If you are birthing a business, then the idea of consistent weekly paychecks has to die. However, what the rebirthing energy brings to you is so much better than what you have said goodbye to, as long as you allow it to grow and thrive. Just like a new baby needs the right food, love, and conditions to grow and thrive, so to do all the other things you birth. If you do not acknowledge the stages, steps, and process of the rebirthing energy, you will stunt the energy in the second chakra, for you will either be focusing only on what you don't want to give up or only be thinking about what you have to gain. Whether we like to admit it or not, bringing new ideas, new energy, new things, and new people into our lives is exciting. We all love bringing new things into our experience, but what we don't like is how that new energy changes our lives, and you can't experience rebirth without change. It is this change that most people will rebel against. You may not even be aware of what energy you are rebelling against in the second chakra. Thank goodness we have a way of checking in.

## EXERCISE
· · · · ·

Grab your tarot deck and start to shuffle. As you shuffle, close your eyes and take a couple of nice, deep breaths. In this respect, the shuffling of the cards is a meditative process. As you breathe and continue to gently shuffle your cards, ask yourself the following question: "What rebirthing energy am I rebelling against?" As you ask, see orange light come up from your second chakra, move through your hands, and infuse with the cards. Once the cards feel energized, fan them out in front of you face down. Ask your question one more time, then select three cards. Your spread will look something like this:

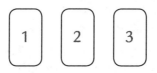

- *Card 1:* What you are rebelling against.
- *Card 2:* Why you think you need to hang on to this energy.
- *Card 3:* What will happen when you let it die.

When you look at these cards, I want you to notice if you automatically assume some cards are good and some cards are bad, and if you think you got bad cards in places you thought you would see good cards. For example, did you get something like the Sun or the Ten of Pentacles for card 2? These cards might make it seem like doubling down and digging in your heels is actually a good thing, but let me ask you this: Is being in the sun all the time good for you, or will it eventually burn you and everything around you to a crisp? What if that Ten of Pentacles costs you something more meaningful, like true love or true connection? Is the price of your rebellion worth it? Now think about getting bad cards like the Ten of Swords, the Three of Swords, or the Tower in the last position. Actually, I think these are fabulous cards to have here, as they show exactly what needs to happen for you to move on from the death of an old, worn-out idea or an unhealthy way of life. I guess what I am saying here is to dig deeper before you decide what cards are having a positive or negative affect on your rebirthing energy, because in chakra work, nothing should ever be taken at face value.

Now that you have explored this rebirthing energy a little, it is time to pull a significator for it. Think about what this energy does, about how it both creates and destroys, and about how it can be in the moment but also stretched out over a long period of time. Cards that would work well here might be Death, Temperance, Ace of Wands, Five of Cups, Eight of Cups, and Queen of Cups. Keep in mind that this card has to align to how you see rebirthing energy working in you. If you already know what card you want as your significator, pull it out of your deck and start doing some journal work with it. If, however, you have no idea what card you want to align to this position, then hold your deck to your heart, take a couple of nice, deep breaths, and steady yourself. Next, fan your cards out face down so you can see them, and hold your hand over the cards just for a couple of seconds. Before you scan them, take another deep breath. Now select your card. We are keeping this card upright, so if you selected it in the reversed aspect, please turn it the other way. Now take your card to your journal and begin your deep dive into your card of birth, death, and rebirth.

· · · · ·

## 3. Grief

If the energy of rebirth is found in the second chakra, then it can't be much of a surprise to see grief down here as well. When things die, we grieve for them, or more to the point, we should. Grief is one of the more complex emotions we deal with as humans. Grief is both an individual and collective process. Grief is intimate and shared, and like most things that blur the lines, we tend not to handle it very well as a society. Instead, we tend to push people through the grief process, which can lead to violence, anger, and hostility. If you have ever lost someone you love, there is a good chance you felt some sort of pressure to get back to life, get over your loss, and pick up where you left off, even though that is impossible, from both an emotional and energetic level. Grief is such an important part of being human. It is what allows us to connect and be connected, not just to ourselves, but to humanity at large. There are no time limits for grief, and in fact, we are constantly in different states of grief throughout any given day. It is natural to grieve, yet we have made it something that we only allow in extreme circumstances and only for as long as it is socially accommodating.

Here in the second chakra, we grieve for everything we have ever had to say goodbye to—people, jobs, animals, clothes that no longer fit, abandoned dreams, and versions of ourselves that never manifested. We are perpetually creating conditions to grieve, which makes perfect sense, since we are also in a constant state of rebirthing. Life, death, and all of death's complicated emotional spin-offs live right here in your second chakra. It is a messy chakra, and as we continue to make our way through this chapter, you will start to see why. However, we need to learn to work with this chakra, embrace all of it, and keep it moving in a healthy and beneficial way. This is why we need to learn about grief. Thankfully, the tarot is prepped and ready to help us, as it holds several cards that are especially designed for this emotion.

Off the top of your head, the tarot card you might automatically say represented grief would be the Three of Swords, but there is also the Five of Cups, the Five of Pentacles, the Tower, Strength, Death, the Devil, the Ten of Swords, the Nine of Wands, the Four of Pentacles, and even the Eight of Cups. All these cards deal with grief in one form or another, because grief is so normal that it continually pops up throughout your tarot deck. You have probably pulled one of the above cards recently and not even connected it to a grief state you may have been experiencing, or maybe one of the above cards has been stalking you, as the cards do when they really want to hammer home a message. If that is the case, which card was it? If you haven't been paying attention to your cards or just can't remember which of these cards has been present recently, don't worry. We are going to do an exercise right now to see which of these grief cards has a message for you.

## EXERCISE

· · · · ·

Grab your deck and start to shuffle slowly, taking nice, deep breaths as you do. Connect to the energy of your second chakra by shifting your attention to the area in your pelvis. As you breathe, see an orange light moving up from your pelvis into your hands and spreading into the cards as you continue to shuffle. When you feel your cards are ready, stop shuffling. Then, just start flipping them over one on top of the other until one of the grief cards mentioned earlier shows up. Stop when you first come across one of those cards. This card is your grief significator. Remove the card, place it in front of you, and put the other cards you flipped over back in the deck. Next, you are going to pull four more cards around this grief card to get a picture of the grief energy that is currently in your life. Your spread will look like this:

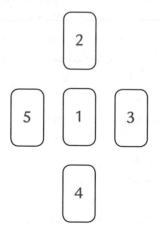

- *Card 1:* Your grief significator.
- *Card 2:* What area of your life this grief pertains to.

- *Card 3:* What support you require to assist you with this grief.
- *Card 4:* The energy being blocked by not allowing yourself to grieve.
- *Card 5:* The gift this grief brings into your life.

Take your time with these cards and allow yourself to sit with them before you even start writing in your journal or try to read them. Just gaze at the images for a few seconds, taking them in as you slowly breathe in and out. Be gentle with your grief and move at your own pace.

When you feel ready, pick up your journal and start making your notes and comments about the cards, starting with the first card, your current grief significator. This card will constantly be changing, but for now, this is your point of focus. Move slowly into card 2 and explore the area of your life this grief has shown up. Is it in your relationships (cups); in your career, money, or health (pentacles); an idea, project, or belief (swords); or a bit of a spiritual crisis (wands)? If you got a court card, know that this could be a person in your life or a part of yourself that you are grieving for. If you have a major arcana card, you may be experiencing a life shift. Move into the third card and allow yourself to be open to the support. See if you can make a commitment to getting more support for your grief work. Card 4 might be a surprise, as you may have had no idea grief was the reason this energy was not flowing. Last, honor the gift, whatever it may be, even if it is a card you don't consider much of a gift.

Once you have journaled all you can, head to your favorite tarot or spiritual books and dig a little deeper. Don't be afraid to stay with this spread for a couple of days or even a couple of weeks. Remember, grief has no time limit, and you can take as long as you want working through its complicated energy.

· · · · ·

## 4. Desire

What is desire? I ask this question a lot, and I get a lot of different answers. Most people think of desire as a sexual energy, and there is no doubt that desire and lust are likely partners in crime. However, not all desire is sexual, and not all sex involves desire. Like most of the issues in the second chakra, desire is complicated, mainly because it tends to be different for each of us. How you experience desire will not be the same as how I experience desire. Things that you strive for while riding the wave of desire won't be the same as your partner's or your kids' or your best friend's. We are not all driven by the same desire energy. Each of us has our own desire triggers, and when we are out of alignment with them, we can cause harm to the second chakra. Desire is not just something we actively experience; it can also be something that is used as a weapon against us. Sexual assault is just one of those forms. Desire tends to also be socially regulated. As women, we are often taught that our desire is not important, that we are merely tools or vessels to fulfill the desires of men, part of living in a patriarchy. This has caused tremendous harm in the second chakra for a lot of women. I have seen many damaged second chakras in women who have been abused, who have been afraid to ask to have their own desires filled, or who have tried to shut down desire altogether. Throughout my work over the decades, I have found that most women, especially those over sixty-five, are uncomfortable discussing desire and will be quick to shut down a conversation when the topic arises.

Yet desire is natural. We all have it in one form or another, and we all need to learn how to explore, experience, and enjoy it. When we understand that the energy of desire is connected to the heart and that it can show up in many different ways, we can take the pressure off our sexual selves. We don't always have to be performing sexual acts to experience desire, since wants and needs can also be very heart-based. However, repairing this area may very well result in sparking your sexual self back to life.

## EXERCISE
. . . . .

There is something in your life that is channeling your desire energy, so what are the things you currently desire? Is it a new job, a new car, a new lover, a vacation, or maybe more money?

Be honest here and know there is no wrong or right answer. Your desires are your own, and you don't have to justify them. Pick up your deck and let's find a significator card that represents your main desire. If it's money, perhaps you want the Ten or King of Pentacles. If it's a new lover, perhaps you want the Lovers, the Two of Cups, or even the Devil. Do you desire fame or more recognition? Then maybe you need the Star or the Six of Wands. Find the card that is right for you, pull it out of the deck, and put it face up in front of you. Then pull a card to answer the following questions:

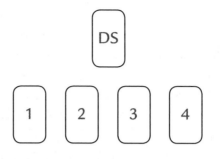

- *DS:* Desire Significator
- *Card 1:* Why do I desire this?
- *Card 2:* What do I think this desire will bring me?
- *Card 3:* What is this desire blocking?
- *Card 4:* What will this desire cost me?

Lay the four cards out in a row under your desire significator and take a good look at the story of your desire. Are you seeing this desire for what it really is, or have you been romanticizing it and how it will make you feel? In other words, are there a lot of cup cards or dreamy cards in your answers? Oftentimes we confuse fantasy for desire, and they are not the same thing. Desire is an energy that drives people toward something that they would not normally do. It starts in the second chakra with your center of creativity and desire, hatching a plan, and is then trumpeted to the heavens through the heart. In many ways, creativity and desire work hand in hand to help us achieve our goals and dreams. Desire pushes us, keeps us motivated, and lights a fire inside us. Can you see that in the cards you have drawn, and are there any wands? If not, then there is a good chance your current source of desire is not serving you, but instead is binding you, especially if you have mainly swords in your answers. This is true also if you have pentacles, which can be heavy and weigh down the energy of your second chakra.

Take your time with these cards and journal with them. Let them talk to you in second-chakra language of desire, wants, and needs. When you have gone as deep as you feel you can, add your sacral chakra significator card and your creativity significator card to the spread.

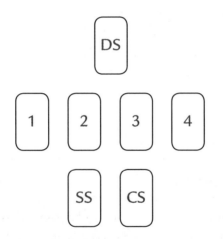

- *SS:* Sacral Chakra Significator
- *CS:* Creativity Significator

This will give you a seven-card spread and show you how your current desire is playing with your center of creativity and how it is affecting the overall well-being of your second chakra. With more cards in the mix, you will have an even better view of what elements are dominating your center of desire. Keep in mind the second chakra is already made of water, so an abundance of water in this spread may mean you are starting to feel pulled down or swept away by your desire energy. What I really want you to focus on is if there is a missing element or one that is so lacking in representation that it may as well not have bothered showing up. This missing or lacking element will hold the key to balancing our desire energy and bringing it into power. Write about this in your journal and think of ways that you could bring more of this element into your wishes, dreams, wants, and needs. If, however, everything seems fairly well rounded, then congratulations! Your center of desire is doing okay.

· · · · ·

## 5. Memory

I know many of you who are familiar with the chakras are looking at this section scratching your head. What on earth is memory doing all the way down here in the sacral chakra? Memory, as we deal with it energetically, holds an emotion that has either caused great pain or great joy. Emotion is what the second chakra is all about. When we do healing work for trauma, we work on the second chakra. When we do healing work for abuse, we do it here in the second chakra, because the waters of the sacral are both deep and expansive. It holds every memory you have had since the time of your conception. It may even hold memories your soul was clinging to before it manifested into the cluster of cells that eventually formed your human body. How we respond to things in our lives depends on what emotional charge we have wrapped that memory in. When you send information to your brain, it searches for a connection, and that connection is kept right here, in the waters of the sacral. That is pretty deep, pardon the pun.

Every time a situation arises in your life, an emotional memory is triggered. This will then send information up to your brain, and you will respond in accordance with that emotional charge. Let me give you an example. Let's say your partner, the love of your life, has a habit of just leaving the house without telling you. They don't say goodbye, they don't give you a hug or a kiss, and they do not acknowledge you in any way. They just up and leave. Now, if you have a memory of being abandoned or neglected, this will trigger your second chakra like a raging storm, and before you know it, this simple act of leaving the house becomes about your partner leaving you, not loving you, or dismissing you. The event will make you view the situation through the lens of your emotional memory. You can see how this might distort your perception of what might really be happening and what you are imagining happening. Hence, because your partner does not share your emotional memory trigger, they will be left wondering what on earth you are getting so upset about. This will end up causing conflict, as you will feel like you are not understood, which will just hook you to that emotional memory even more, dragging you deeper and deeper into the murky waters of the sacral. Things can spiral out of control pretty quickly.

Through my work with clients, I have learned they usually are not fully aware of what emotional memory hook they are viewing the world through. This is why I am such an advocate for therapy and energy work, because we are just too close to ourselves to see how we have bent our perceptions. Thankfully, tarot also gives us a way to explore this issue as well.

## EXERCISE

· · · · ·

Grab your deck and start slowly and gently shuffling the cards. Take some nice, slow breaths and see that orange light in your pelvis. As you take each breath, see the orange light expanding upward and coming up into your arms and down into your hands, where it now infuses with your tarot cards. Just visualize this orange sacral light filling up your deck and turning each of your cards into an emotional memory. Relax into your shuffling, and when you feel your cards are filled with enough energy, stop and fan them out in front of you face down. Take a deep, cleansing breath, gently move your hand over the cards, and ask the following question: "What emotional memory am I currently viewing my life through?" When you find a card that feels warm or cold or makes your hand tingle, flip it over, and make sure you have it in the reversed aspect. Yes, this card needs to be upside down. It's a topsy-turvy issue, so we need a topsy-turvy card.

What card did you select?

This card is the current significator for your memory issues in the second chakra, and it is the card that is influencing you right now and your interactions with the world around you. Spend some time with this card, take it to your journal, and answer the following three questions:

1. How is this card a gift?
2. How is this card a burden?
3. Is this card true or imagined?

There is a reason you and this card are currently having a journey together, and it will help you to explore that journey in its positive and negative forms. It is also important to answer the final question, which is "Is this card true or imagined?" This question is really asking you if this card is actually happening in your life or if you are just imagining it playing out on your life screen. It is important to see if you are allowing emotional memory to trick you. For the most part you are, but not all the time. The three questions are not easy to answer, and if you feel like you need more information from the cards, pull a card for each of them and journal those as well.

Once you have done the journaling exercise and feel you have a better grasp on this issue, memory, or perception, meditate on it. Just do a small, simple meditation in which you see the issues you journaled about being washed out of the second chakra. See the waters of your sacral chakra clean, calm, and free of this issue. Watch as the light dances across the water of your second chakra, skipping and playing, as a light breeze brushes against your skin, making you feel peaceful and calm. See yourself sitting at the water's edge admiring your memories, knowing that you can release any and all of them whenever you wish. Smile as you do this meditation so that you can make new emotional memories, filled with gratitude and love. Memories are what you make of them, and here at the water's edge of the sacral chakra, make them life affirming so that they can effortlessly assist you in vibrational growth and expansion.

· · · · ·

## 6. Pleasure

I feel it's important to start this section describing the difference between pleasure and desire. For one thing, desire is something we wish to experience, whereas pleasure is how we allow ourselves to experience it. Desire drives creativity, and pleasure is how we engage with that journey. Pleasure, much like desire, however, is not something a lot of women are taught, and they are instead trained that they are a vehicle for someone else's pleasure. It is this suppression of our natural pleasure state that does damage to the second chakra. By denying ourselves pleasure, we can stifle the energy that moves in and out of this chakra, and this can lead to all sorts of sexual problems, not to mention it can severely damage how we engage with positive experiences in our life. Our ability to explore, engage, and experience pleasure trickles up to the rest of the chakra pillar, creeping its way into every aspect of our lives. That is how important pleasure is.

Let's get one thing out of the way first, pleasure is a sexual energy, but that doesn't mean sex is the only way to experience it. Pleasure activates the healing sexual energy of the second chakra, which is energy that does positive and life-affirming work in and throughout our bodies. We are sexual beings, even if we don't participate in the act of sex, and playing with pleasure allows us to keep that energy active and flowing. Desire may let you know what turns you on, but pleasure is all about allowing yourself to take that feeling over the edge into a state of bliss, harmony, peace, and creativity. You could say pleasure is the orgasm center of the second chakra. I can always tell the state of someone's relationship with pleasure by the way they react to the Devil card. There seem to be only two responses people have when they see the Devil card come up in tarot. They either see that card as something that liberates them or something that binds them. That is also how people see pleasure, either as a form of freedom and expression or as a gateway to sin.

## EXERCISE
· · · · ·

Let's pull the Devil card out of your deck and do some journaling on how you view the role of the Devil in your life, and how you respond to it when it shows up in a reading. As you begin to write out your responses to the Devil card, consider starting your statements with "I am the one who ..." For example, you might write, "I am the one who is bound by all of my mistakes," "I am the one who sees the world as a smorgasbord and does not feel guilty about exploring it," "I am the one who feels repressed and full of shame," or "I am the one who feels liberated and free to be who I am." Write as many "I am" statements as you can while you do your journal work. The statements you write here will give you an insight into how you are allowing yourself to experience pleasure. You either see it as something that hooks you to guilt, shame, and judgment, or you see it as an energy that frees you to experience the world without being hooked at all.

When you have done all you can with the Devil card alone, let's build a spread around him and take a closer look at how pleasure, desire, and creativity are driving the energy inside your second chakra. Place these cards as follows in front of you in a simple three-card spread:

| 1 | 2 | 3 |

- *Card 1:* Desire Significator
- *Card 2:* Creativity Significator
- *Card 3:* The Devil

Now, let's take it one step further. Pick up the rest of your deck, leaving the three cards lined up in front of you, and give them a shuffle. Take a couple of nice, deep breaths as you focus on the Devil card. Let the energy of the Devil dance into your cards as you gently shuffle them. Take another deep breath and ask the following question: "How can the Devil teach me to engage more actively with pleasure in my life?" Visualize the question going into the cards as you shuffle, and when you feel ready, fan the cards out in front of you face down and select a card. Place this card directly on top of the Devil card.

The card you have selected is showing you the end result of activating your desire, creativity, and pleasure. This card is also going to become your pleasure significator card. Now don't get upset or put off if you happened to get a card like the Tower, the Three of Swords, Death, the Five of Cups, or any other card that you may not be happy to see. Know that this is okay, correct, and still a good sign. In energy work we do not expect everything to be roses, butterflies, and unicorns. It's kind of the point that there are things that will come up for healing, and pleasure may be that area for you. Just sit with your card and view it from a point of nonjudgment. This is a lesson card, a card that brings with it illumination, and it will open the door to something amazing if you allow it to. If, on the other hand, you got an amazing card, fabulous.

Take this spread to your journal and explore it further. If something has presented itself for healing—and you will know this if it makes you uncomfortable—then write about how working through this block, pain point, or trigger will free up your center of pleasure and allow you to more deeply engage in playing with desire and creativity. If something came up to be celebrated, then journal about that, as it is always important to praise our good work and acknowledge our personal wins. Keep your words kind, compassionate, and loving, and you will be well on your way to moving healing energy in and around your second chakra.

• • • • •

## 7. The Past

Considering this chakra is where memory, grief, and death live, it should not be a surprise that the second chakra is predominately influenced by events of the past. The present may live in the root, but the past lives only one door up. This is one of the traps of the second chakra. It can keep you hooked to a life, to a world, to a version of yourself that no longer exists. It can create fears, doubts, and paralysis from events that are long gone, and it can stop you from embracing the here and now. As chakras go, the second one is pretty heavy. I guess we should not expect anything less from the emotional center of the body. Living your life from a past energy experience means you will never truly grow, and opportunities to thrive will be missed or ignored. You will create a version of yourself that is always either trying to recreate something or trying to escape something. The past is a murky place, where ghosts of the former versions of our lives haunt the emotion-lined shore of our sacral lake. Who you were then is no help to who you are now. What you used to do, or how you used to act or react, is not helpful to what needs to be done in this moment. What has happened is long dead, and you can only ever deal with what is currently happening.

We all allow our past to influence us in some ways. We all have moments when we hang on to some pain or wound that has been inflicted upon us, be it as simple as being stuck in bad traffic or being betrayed by a friend or lover. We offer rent to these situations in our mind and give this energy permission to contaminate the entire chakra system. Some of us don't allow this energy to linger for long: we become aware of where our mind is and we take steps to shift feelings and emotions, moving ourselves back into the moment. This, for the most part, is the natural cycle of dealing with an emotional charge. We sit in it for a short period of time and then move on. Sometimes, however, we let that energy take up permanent residency and give it permission to drive the bus of our lives into a very long and dark tunnel.

There are cards in the tarot that let us know right away if we are living in a past emotional state, and the ones that stick out in my mind include the Four of Pentacles, the Devil, the Tower, the Ten of Swords, the Knight of Cups, the Six of Cups, the Nine of Swords, and the Ten of Wands. When these cards show up in a reading, you can get a sense of how the past is influencing things around a person. The Ten of Swords lets me know a situation has moved on but the querent has not. The Ten of Wands shows someone literally carrying their past around with them. The tarot is wise in the ways it alerts us to how deep the waters of our past have become.

## EXERCISE

· · · · ·

Now it is time to select a significator for your past. Choose a card that is a visual cue that you have your head behind you and are not focused on what's in front of you. This card may have an image you connect with, or perhaps you are connecting to the meaning of the card. Either way is fine, as long as the card will always prompt you to know you are being influenced by the past. Consider using one of the cards listed in the previous paragraph. Once you have your card, lay it face up in front of you in the reversed aspect. Yes, this card needs to be upside down, even if you didn't draw it that way. Just take a few nice, deep breaths before you pick up your journal. If possible, see if you can identify the past emotional charge that this card triggers in you as you view it. Write these emotions down as they pop up. Circle the very first one on your list, as this is the one that may very well be driving your emotions. Keep writing until you feel you have emptied the well of triggers or responses to the card.

Now, let's go back to the first memory or past experience you listed, the one you circled, and explore it further by pulling a card for the following questions:

- *S:* Past Significator
- *Card 1:* How does this past emotional charge hook me?
- *Card 2:* What is this past energy blocking?
- *Card 3:* How do I release this emotional charge?
- *Card 4:* What will I feel like when I let it go?

As you shuffle, visualize an orange light coming up from your second chakra, moving up through your body and into your arms. See this light, as it moves down your arms and into your fingers, slowly infusing the cards you shuffle in your hands. Move the cards slowly and keep your breath nice and steady. Focus on only one question at a time, and see it as it writes itself on the screen of your mind. Once the question is fully formed in your mind's eye, fan your cards out face down and select a card for your question. Repeat this process until you have all four cards. You should now have five cards in total lined up in front of you, your past significator card and the four cards you chose in response to your four questions:

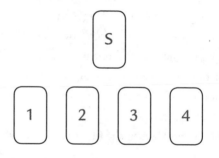

Take these cards to your journal and spend some time with them. Really be open to how the past may be influencing the decisions you make and the way you are currently living your life. Write off the top of your head first, then dig deeper into your tarot books. Allow this exploration into your reading to help you see the triggers finally unhooking from you and allowing the past to drop away. This small exercise will move a lot of energy through your second chakra as it releases toxins from the past emotional energy you are working on, so make sure to ground afterward and drink plenty of water to flush your kidneys. When you are done with your journal work and are fully hydrated, just close out this section by placing your hands on your pelvis and sending your sacral chakra some loving energy. You can say the words "I love you" out loud or just imagine loving energy pumping out of your palms and into your sacral chakra. This will help ground you and assist in balancing out any and all energy you have shifted in this chapter.

• • • • •

## Sacral Chakra Tarot Healing

Now that you have worked through the seven key issues of the second chakra, it is time to do some energy healing work on all that you have discovered, all that has bubbled up, and all that has presented itself for cleaning and clearing. Grab your tarot deck and get out the significator cards for the issues covered in this chapter. Select your significator card for the sacral chakra and place it in front of you. This card is going to be the middle card in your sacral chakra healing mandala wheel.

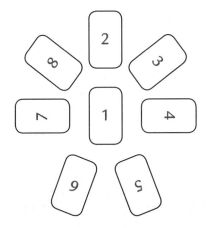

Your card order is as follows:

- *Card 1:* Sacral Chakra Significator
- *Card 2:* Creativity Significator
- *Card 3:* Birth and Rebirth Significator
- *Card 4:* Grief Significator
- *Card 5:* Desire Significator
- *Card 6:* Memory Significator
- *Card 7:* Pleasure Significator
- *Card 8:* The Past Significator

Your center card is going to be the energy you will see flowing in and out of the other cards, as if a beautiful orange smoke wisps out of the card and starts to tickle the other cards around it. As we move into the visualization part of this exercise, move your hands over the cards as you say the following affirmations for each of the cards surrounding your sacral chakra significator. The tarot mandala helps anchor your energy healing work and allows you to engage more fully with the overall process. Your affirmations are as follows:

- *Card 2:* I am a creative person.
- *Card 3:* I am constantly birthing new energy into my life.
- *Card 4:* I am allowing myself to grieve for things when they end.
- *Card 5:* I am actively seeking things I desire.
- *Card 6:* I am improving my memory each and every day.
- *Card 7:* I am allowing myself to seek and enjoy pleasure.
- *Card 8:* I am learning to use the past as a tool to move myself forward in my present everyday life.

Find somewhere comfortable and quiet, where you won't be disturbed for up to twenty minutes. Place your cards where you can see them and start rubbing your palms gently together as you focus on your breathing. Rub your hands together for about forty seconds, activating the energy centers in your palms. You might start to feel some heat in your hands, and this is good. Now place your hands on your pelvic area and focus on your breath, inhaling through your nose. Feel the breath as it hits the back of your throat, fills your lungs, and expands your belly. As you exhale from the mouth, feel the breath leaving your body and notice the depression of the abdomen. Let the breath work become automatic, and shift your focus to your cards, starting with the center card, which is your sacral chakra significator. Visualize the orange smoke gently rising from the card and twirling around the wheel you have created around it. Each time you exhale, the smoky wisps extend farther and farther. Sit like this for a few minutes, just doing the breath work and keeping your hands on your pelvic area as you feel your chest rise and fall, and visualize the smoky orange energy infusing your spread.

When you feel ready, move your hands to your tarot mandala and move them along each card as you speak the corresponding affirmation statements out loud. Read through the entire list three times. Once you have finished, just relax and focus on the breath work, placing the hands back on your knees. As you inhale, feel the smoky orange energy coming into your nose, hitting the back of your throat, filling up your lungs and moving into the base of your pelvis, infusing the sacral chakra. Relax into this, as you inhale all this lovely infused energy, and let this energy clean and clear your sacral chakra as it embeds your affirmations into your chakra. When this feels complete, remove your hands and just breathe normally for thirty to forty seconds. Thank your cards, and you are done.

You can repeat this simple tarot healing session anytime you want, and by all means, journal about how the session made you feel or any revelations you had during the session. The more you know, the more you inquire, the more you heal.

**3**

# The Solar Plexus Chakra

In chapter 1, we learned how we consider ourselves in relation to the world around us. In chapter 2, we took a look at how we perceive that world through our emotional body. Both chapter 1 and chapter 2 deal with what happens inside us, but here in chapter 3 we change gears and start to actively engage with the energy outside us. Think of it this way: in the first two chapters of this book we played inside the house, and now we are headed outside to play in the streets. Where the root and sacral are more solitary chakras, the solar plexus needs friends. It is our center for social activity, and it very much thrives on a steady diet of interactions and engagement with people who are not us. In this chapter you are going to explore seven issues the solar plexus deals with on a consistent and ongoing basis. Just like the previous two chapters, these seven issues each have their own section in this chapter, as they all have important information for you regarding the health and well-being of your solar plexus chakra.

The sections are as follows:

1. Self-Expression
2. Empowerment
3. Worthiness
4. Play
5. Engagement
6. Rebellion
7. Action

## Manipura

The solar plexus chakra, *manipura* in Sanskrit, in many respects is where we learn identity. However, we do not learn it in the same way we learn it in the root, because here it is about how we show up, who we choose to be, and how we want to play with everyone else as we share in this wonderful dream we call life. When you ask a child what they want to be when they grow up, you are asking them a solar plexus question. This is the same as when we ask adults questions about what they want to do with their lives, what sort of career path they want to have, or how they intend to enter the next phase or decade of their lives. These are all solar plexus questions.

The solar plexus energy center controls your stomach, upper intestine, digestive system, liver, pancreas, spleen, and gallbladder. Things are constantly changing in this energy center, and unlike the lower two chakras, the solar plexus is always up for reinvention. The third chakra is mutable, constantly in motion. It likes to be entertained and finds consistency boring. We are always doing a bit of a juggling act in the solar plexus. We work with who we think we are in the root, who we feel we should be creating in the sacral, and who we really want to be in the solar plexus. The solar plexus knows us; it gets us and wants us to express our authenticity out into the world.

Problems only occur when the self in the solar plexus wants to express itself and is out of alignment with who we see ourselves to be in the first and second chakras. When the bottom two chakras are not on the same page with the third chakra, all hell breaks loose, and your body becomes a war zone. Like all wars, there are no winners, only those who get left to deal with the chaos and devastation that has been left behind.

Who is the you who lives in your third chakra? Let's find out.

## EXERCISE
· · · · ·

To select a significator for your solar plexus, only use the court cards. You can choose this card one of two ways. If you already have a good idea about what your true inner self looks like, you can just select the court card that is aligned with that vision. If, however, you are not sure, because this is something you truly struggle with (and I include myself in this category), remove the court cards from your deck and give them a shuffle. Fan them out in front of you and ask this question: "Who is the me who lives inside my third chakra?" See the question form in your mind and gently scan the cards with your fingertips. When you feel a card that either heats up, is cool to the touch, or vibrates in some way, flip that card over. You will have to trust that this version of you is desperate to be expressed via the solar plexus at this time. Take your card to your journal and start writing about how this court card archetype is both similar to and different from who you see as yourself. Think about the activities, jobs, and social circles your court archetype would engage in, and then write if these are things you are currently doing or would like to do. As you journal with this card, really dig deep into the life this member of the court would have. Think about it in terms of your own and see what opportunities await you as you start to embrace this version of who you are, or who you are becoming, as you get ready to work with the energy of your solar plexus.

· · · · ·

## 1. Self-Expression

The term *self-expression* has become a bit of a buzzword over the last couple of decades. Be who you want to be, let your true self shine, and all that crap. The problem is, despite the very nice marketing campaigns around self-expression, society at large does not want you to be anything other than the tidy box they have imagined for you. Still today, being gay, transgender, nonbinary, or any other form of nonheteronormative expression is still very much frowned upon. Self-expression can include anything from how you dress, to how you present yourself to the outside world, to how you think, create, work, talk, walk, and so on. If you have ever heard someone say, "I do this because it is part of who I am," they are speaking third-chakra language. Most people do things because their family wanted them to or there was an expectation from someone outside of themselves. I hear this from clients a lot. They ended up in careers or jobs their family expected them to pursue and now find themselves lost, disconnected, and sick. This can cause damage in the third chakra, which can lead to all sorts of digestive issues.

When we try to fit into someone else's mold, we do damage to our bodies—vibrationally at first, then physically. Your physical body is part of your self-expression, and as a society we are continually being told how that body should look, who will admire it, and how we should manage it if we wish to be accepted. Think of the number of women who suffer from eating disorders, the rise of fad diets, and the ever-present body shaming that happens online on a regular basis. With all the outside noise beating us around the head on a consistent basis, it is no wonder so many struggle with this third chakra issue. It would be wonderful to get to a point where we see who we are as an ever-changing character in a play, one who can switch and change at a moment's notice and one who is not tied down to being any one thing at any given time. It would also be wonderful to be free to express ourselves on a daily, hourly, and moment-to-moment basis with confidence, ease, and grace. This is what the solar plexus craves and is the energy we work very hard to create during our healing, which is why having a self-expression significator can be so important to the healing process.

## EXERCISE
. . . . .

Although you are free to use any card in your tarot deck as your self-expression significator, keep in mind that the court cards are the people of the tarot. They do show very distinct forms of self-expression, and I should point out that there is nothing wrong with wanting to be a king, queen, or knight or to show up in a childlike manner. The most important thing about this card is that it shows how you want to see yourself, the you liberated from labels and expectations, the inner you who would love to be free to play in the bigger outside world. You can select this card on purpose or do it intuitively. Once you have this card, I want you to make a decision about whether or not you feel you have this card upside down or upright. If you feel you are working toward bringing this version of yourself to the forefront and are confident you are making strides, keep the card in its upright aspect. If, however, you struggle with this version of yourself and have fear and anxiety over letting this you out into the world, flip your card and work with it in the reversed aspect, as this will more accurately represent how this energy is currently being circulated around the third chakra.

Take this card to your journal in whatever aspect you have decided it will be for now. Write with this card for as long as you feel you have words. Talk about how you are making this version of yourself a reality or why you feel you struggle with allowing this inner you out in the world. Be honest about how you feel in your journal work, as it is a sacred space for you to find points of healing. You will either pour words onto the page or struggle to get a few sentences. This is all normal, and if you are struggling, pick up your tarot books and see if something in them helps you connect more with your card. Look for key words such as *authentic, true self, vibrational alignment, manifesting,* and of course *self-expression.*

Once you have finished your journal work, use this card in a form of meditation by seeing yourself and the card become one. Visualize yourself as the person in the card, such as seeing yourself wearing their clothes, living their lives, and feeling as free as possible. Watch as you laugh, play, and move through the world of the card without fear. Allow this new energy to settle into your solar plexus. You may even be inclined to place your hand over your chakra point, just above your naval, and feel it warm up as you keep infusing it with your wonderful meditation. Do this meditation as often as you feel called, and return to the journal work if you also feel the nudge to write. This is all about you being comfortable with you, so do the energy healing work for as long, or as little, as you like. You can also add crystals, essential oils, and other modalities as you go along. Just be you and embrace the call of who you are, as this is all the solar plexus really wants for you anyway.

· · · · ·

## 2. Empowerment

The solar plexus is our center of power. It is where we pull energy from the lower chakras together and channel them into raw energy. If our lower chakras are in good health, we feel strong, capable, and empowered, but if our lower chakras are a hot mess, we feel weak, afraid, and disempowered. It is here in the solar plexus where we will double down on our belief that the world is either against us or with us. Either we will be able to happily and quickly manifest things we need and want, or we will be constantly complaining that nothing ever goes right and our lives are one giant problem that is not capable of being solved. My wife's meditation teacher, who is a Buddhist monk, tells her all the time to focus on the solar plexus in order to put her attention into being present with her raw energy. When we are present with our raw power, we drop the need to be separate from all that is around us and in us. Instead, we feel whole, connected, and empowered. You may have also heard the saying that someone "has fire in their belly." That saying has nothing to do with indigestion but is about having the power to be courageous, determined, and strategic, which are all words of the solar plexus. I always think of the solar plexus as a place where all my tarot knights live. Sometimes they are armed and ready for battle, making plans and getting things into order so they don't feel overwhelmed. Other times they are pulling creative energy up from the sacral chakra and manifesting amazing things, and yet other times they are asleep and completely at peace.

How we feel about our place in our own lives affects how this energy center works. If we feel disempowered, we can find ourselves telling a victim story and using thoughts, feelings, and language that will dramatically erode and damage our third chakra. This energy can harm the stomach, the digestive system, and the liver. Disempowerment often brings with it anger, and anger produces heat inside the body, raising acid levels. I guess fire in the belly really could be indigestion. There is no doubt that in order to have a healthy, functioning solar plexus we need to feel empowered—not all the time, but most of the time. We need to feel some sense of peace and power in our lives. We need to feel more at ease and less overwhelmed. We need to be drawing up that energy of connection from the root chakra so we can unleash our creative problem-solving energy in the sacral chakra and mix it here with our raw power.

It sounds like a simple three-step process, right?

Let's see how these three energies are playing together.

## EXERCISE
· · · · ·

First, you are going to need to select a significator for your center of empowerment. This card needs to make you feel strong, confident, and capable, such as the Magician, the High Priestess, the Emperor, any of the court cards, the Eight of Pentacles, the Six of Wands, the Ten of Cups, and even the Hanged Man. Once you have selected your card, lay it face up in front of you. If you wish to journal with this card before you move on to the next step, go right ahead. Come back to the next step when you feel more connected to your card. Next, gather your significator for your area of connection from the root chapter and your significator card for your center of creativity from the solar plexus chapter. We are going to arrange them into a three-card spread in the following order:

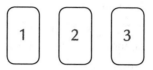

- *Card 1:* Connection Significator
- *Card 2:* Creativity Significator
- *Card 3:* Empowerment Significator

These three cards tell a visual story of how energy is moving upward from the root into the third chakra. This is a pictogram of your three-step empowerment process. For the sake of this exercise, I want you to do this spread a couple of different ways, so make sure you read this part carefully.

- *Spread Version 1:* Put all the cards in the upright aspect.
- *Spread Version 2:* Put all the cards in the reversed aspect.

- *Spread Version 3:* Put the connection card and empowerment card in the reversed aspect and the creativity card in the upright aspect.
- *Spread Version 4:* Put the connection card and the empowerment card in the upright aspect and the creativity card in the reversed aspect.

Why so many variations? It is because each of these will give you a totally different reading, and, most importantly, this is how your energy flip-flops throughout the day. One moment you feel connected, the next you don't. You might feel like you could conquer the world in the morning, but come midafternoon you just want to go back to bed and forget the world exists. Knowing how this energy visually looks can help you start to identify how your energy is working in your outside world quickly and efficiently. This then lets you self-correct without effort or struggle. Knowing which of your significator cards needs some downtime can also stop you from trying to push through periods of your day, or life, that just require you to sit, wait, and show yourself some kindness. You might even start to notice a pattern in which a particular version of the spread continually shows up. This could be key to healing whichever of those cards finds themselves in the reversed aspect. Knowledge is power, and power is the solar plexus's BFF.

· · · · ·

### 3. Worthiness

If you own your own business, freelance, have ever asked for a raise, or have tried to manifest something beyond your current abundance level, you will have bumped up against this issue in your third chakra. Every time a money discussion comes up, you activate this issue inside the solar plexus. The irony is that this chakra has nothing to do with money at all. Worthiness is an imagined concept we have created by deciding what sort of value we offer to the world around us, which is insane. No one human has more value than another. We are all worthy, and none of us can adequately create a number that is the label of our value. Yet we all do this every single day, because we live in a material world where goods and services are bought, sold, and traded on a regular basis. This means we are constantly being asked what we are worth. Numbers begin to haunt us, and we see them in our bank accounts, on our clothes, on the scale, as social media followers, in our paychecks, and in monthly and quarterly reports. Our worth is always seemingly being valued against a set of made-up or imaginary numbers. I should point out this is not a modern concept. We have been deciding the fate of humans based on their value for thousands of years. It is no wonder this has become so embedded into the larger consciousness of society.

How we see our level of worthiness effects the third chakra in a couple of different ways. It can slow it down, giving us less energy throughout the day, making us sluggish and unmotivated. It can also cause the solar plexus chakra to pull past emotional energy up from the sacral chakra and create stress, acid, and anxiety in the digestive system. As someone who owns their own business, I rub up against this issue several times a day. Usually, it doesn't bother me too much, as I understand it is just a figment of my imagination, and the numbers don't mean anything. However, other times those numbers feel like they are holding me hostage. Income needs to be greater than output, and when it is not, you don't have much of a business—in fact, you won't have much of a material life either. These thoughts trigger our safety, security, and stability issues in the root chakra, and then they all join hands and sing songs of your unworthiness around the lake of all your failures in the second chakra.

In order to be rid of the song of shame, you adjust the numbers, oftentimes creeping out of what you imagine your worth to actually be. This is where things can start to fall apart even more. Before we are able to constantly push those numbers or manifest larger and larger things, our sense of worth needs to also grow, and not just the imagined value in our heads. We need to feel our soul value throughout our whole body. This is the raw worthiness that sits in the third chakra, the one free of measurements, and the worthiness that is created just by you being you, the one that is constantly saying, "I *am* enough." Marisa Peer, the founder of Rapid Transformational Therapy, believes that saying "I *am* enough" multiple times a day will change our lives. She believes in this so much that she not only wrote a book about it, she created a movement.[4] This movement is working directly with the third chakra, and it is teaching people all over the world the raw soul value they have just for existing. "I *am* enough" is not tied to anything you do; it is just about you being you. That's it, that's all.

## EXERCISE
· · · · ·

Let's get a visual for your worthiness. Grab your deck and find your worthiness significator card. This card

4. Marisa Peer, *I Am Enough: Mark Your Mirror and Change Your Life* (self-published, 2018).

should align to how you want to vibrate your worthiness into the world. This card may not be how you feel right now, but it is the card you want to vibrationally align to and model yourself after and whose "I *am* enough" energy you want to infuse your third chakra with. Some cards to consider for this might be Temperance, the Aces, the Empress, the Star, the Lovers, the Two of Cups, or even the Three of Pentacles. When you have selected your card, take it to your journal and spend some time with it. Contemplate journaling on the following questions:

- What story would I need to stop telling in order to truly feel this level of worthiness?
- How would embracing the energy of this card change my day-to-day experience?
- Why would I want to feel more worthy?
- Where are the spaces and places in my life that I need to activate the energy of this card first?

If you feel drawn to do so, you can also pull some cards on the questions. You do not need to, as the questions can just be asked of your significator card, but it might help you build a more expansive picture of how this issue of worthiness is affecting your current experience. The images on the cards let us see things we would normally miss. Lined up in a row, the cards tell a very distinct story of how we navigate an issue. We can even talk our way along the row, as if we are retelling a narrative from a picture book. Regardless of how you choose to work with the questions, you will still shift energy in your third chakra just by answering them. Byron Katie, spiritual and mindfulness teacher, teaches in her book *A Mind at Home with Itself* that liberation from the dream, what we think is true, can always be found in inquiry, meaning the more questions we ask, the more we move out of the dream.[5] Perceptions of worthiness based on imagined numbers is a dream, which I would be more than happy to be liberated from, and perhaps you would too.

· · · · ·

## 4. Play

Out of all the issues we explore in the third chakra, this is the one that is possibly the most important of them all. Play is the best thing we can do for our third chakra. Thirty minutes of playtime a day could be the difference between a happy, healthy solar plexus and an unhappy, reactive solar plexus. The great thing about play is that it means something different to everyone. For some people it will be getting dirty, playing sports, rolling in the grass, or even spending time with their young children or grandchildren. For others it might be music, dancing, painting, or some other form of artistic play. However, some of us might see play as a much gentler pursuit, such as coloring, reading, writing, knitting, or even cooking. It is really not important how you play; it only matters that you do, because here in the solar plexus sits the energy of the inner child. It is here that your inner child gets to heal, express himself or

---

5. Byron Katie and Stephen Mitchell, *A Mind at Home with Itself: How Asking Four Questions Can Free Your Mind, Open Your Heart, and Turn Your World Around* (New York: HarperOne, 2017).

herself, and be a cheerleader for your adult self. Inner child work is third chakra work. There is no getting away from that, and play is the best way to heal, engage, and rejoice in your inner child energy.

## EXERCISE
· · · · ·

The inner child work is so important that it even gets a few cards in the tarot, including the pages. The pages remind us to connect with the childlike energy of each suit, to see each element through the lens of a child and explore it as a child would. Remove the pages from your deck and lay them out in front of you face up. Grab your journal and a pen as well. Let's start with the Page of Pentacles, which reminds us to see our material world, including our bodies, as we did when we were children. Do you remember any significant things that happened in your childhood that might be influencing you now as an adult in terms of money, your body, your health, or your ability to have things you want? Sit with this question and close your eyes, taking a few deep breaths before you write down your answers. Once you have written all you can for the Page of Pentacles, let's move on to the Page of Swords. Do you remember any significant incidents in your childhood that made you question your learning abilities? Think about your school experience and maybe things teachers or other adults said to you that have influenced how you have approached learning and even perhaps further education as an adult. Just sit with the question for a moment before you answer. Once you have written all you can for the Page of Swords, let's move on to the Page of Cups. Do you recall how emotions were dealt with in your family? Were they talked about, expressed, or stuffed away where no one could see them? If possible, write about a specific time in your childhood that has influenced how you deal with emotional situations as an adult. Take your time answering these questions, and make sure you have written all you can before moving on. Last, let's look at the Page of Wands. How was religion dealt with in your home, and how has it impacted the way you now engage with and view the world around you?

I am sure you have written some very illuminating answers to the above questions, and I am certain you will be able to ponder over the information for days to come. You might also see where you stopped or stifled your ability or willingness to play. Don't judge any of the information that arose from your inquiry. Just let it be what it is: words on a page in your journal.

The next part of this inner child work is to select the page that seems to require the most healing. This will be the one that caused you discomfort in the exercise. Place this page in the reversed aspect, as this is the energy that your inner child is in need of cleaning and clearing. This card will be your play significator. Like most things in the third chakra, it will change over time, but right now this is the energy you need to get flowing. This is the part of your inner child that is in the most pain. This is blocking your ability to play and engage with the lighter and more joyful parts of your life. Here is the good news: the key to turning that card back up the right way is through play. Your healing map for your inner child should include games, adventures, playdates, and time with special friends. Your wounded page will need this in order to see the world with wonder again. It doesn't matter which page you are working with, play will always be the answer.

Keep your reversed page in front of you, and pick up the rest of your deck. Hold the cards in your hands and visualize a yellow light coming up from your solar plexus into your chest, down your arms, and into your hands. Start to shuffle your deck and see the yellow light infusing the cards. Breathe gently and keep shuffling until you feel the deck is infused enough with solar plexus energy. Fan the cards out in front of you face down and ask the following question: "How can I play today?" Let your hand gently scan the cards and wait for a sensation to prickle on up through your fingertips. Select your card, turn it over, and place it on top of your page. This is the message your page has for you. It is how you can find a way to be playful and more lighthearted in your day, even if the card seems heavy. Remember, you are seeing this card through the eyes of your inner child, not through the lens of your adult experiences. Even cards like the Three of Swords can be made into a game, and you just have to see it that way. You can repeat this one-card draw on a daily basis if you so choose. Trust yourself to know when you have relearned how to connect with the energy of play to heal and engage your inner child. Your solar plexus will thank you for it.

· · · · ·

## 5. Engagement

Engagement is often confused with experience, but they are not the same at all. For the sake of this chapter I am defining experience as something you have and engagement as how much you participate in the experience. By this, I mean how much of the experience do you connect with and allow into your energy, and how much of yourself do you give to an experience at any given time? Another way of thinking about it is to ask yourself if you are showing up to the game of life but sitting on the sidelines or if you are actively participating in the game. The solar plexus chakra needs you to do more than just show up. It needs you to be a focused, committed, and a receptive participant in your own life. But life is busy and it seems impossible to engage with all of it. We have to-do lists that go on for miles. We have jobs, careers, kids, grandkids, partners, spouses, businesses, and so many other things that we cram into a twenty-four-hour period. It is not surprising that we have started to equate showing up with engagement. We have all been guilty of saying, "I'm here," like that was all we were ever meant to do. The third chakra is the action center of your chakra system, which means now that you are here, we would like you to do something, like engage in the experience you have shown up for.

This then begs the question, if you were 10 percent more engaged in your life right now, what would it look like?

## EXERCISE
· · · · ·

You know what's fabulous about your tarot deck? You can draw some cards and visually see where you are deeply engaging in your life and where you are just showing up and then staying on the sidelines. This spread will show what your level of engagement is in your current life. This is a ten-card spread, which is a lot of cards, but we want a full picture of how you are participating in the life you move through each and every day. Lay the cards out as follows:

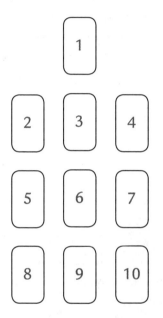

- *Card 1:* Level of engagement with yourself. Just how much are you giving yourself? This card will let you know if you are giving yourself time, space, and attention.

- *Card 2:* Level of engagement with your body. This card will let you know how your health and overall well-being are going. When we engage with our bodies, we become invested in them. We don't talk negatively to our bodies or feel like they are enemy number one. Instead, we want them to be healthy, pain-free, mobile, and active. This card will allow you to see how your relationship with your body is faring.

- *Card 3:* Level of engagement with your mind. Your mind needs constant attention, for if it is not growing through learning, it is slowly dying. This card will show you if your mind is active, excited, and still very much expanding, or if you have become lazy and stopped trying to learn new things or create new habits.

- *Card 4:* Level of engagement with your spirit. This card might be a bit of a smack in the face for some of you. It is easy to say we are spiritual beings, but it is another to be fully engaged with spirit on daily basis. This card will show you how your relationship with spirit is faring, how receptive you are to bringing spirit into your life, and how trusting you are that it is even there at all.

- *Card 5:* Level of engagement with your spouse or partner. It's easy to tune out when you are in a long-term relationship. It is also easy to forget that you are not the only person in the relationship. This card will let you know how you are playing your part in your partnership, if you are truly being aware and present, and if you are actively participating in making your relationship strong, safe, and stable.

- *Card 6:* Level of engagement with your family. This card will let you know if you are overinvolved or underinvolved in both your immediate and extended families. For the most part, people are overly engaged, and this takes time and energy away from other areas of their lives. Be mindful with whatever card shows up here.

• *Card 7:* Level of engagement with your friends. Just like family, it can be easy to overengage in the lives of our friends. At some point, you will need to find balance here, so pay attention to the card that shows up in this position.

• *Card 8:* Level of engagement with your money. This card will let you know how your relationship with money is going. This is a pretty important relationship and one you really should be actively engaged in, as it benefits not only you but everyone else as well.

• *Card 9:* Level of engagement with your job. This card will let you see how much you participate in the creative part of your life. Your job, career, or business is a huge part of your life. You spend most of your time here, which means that how you engage here will have implications in the rest of your chakra system.

• *Card 10:* Level of engagement with your goals and dreams. Most people like the idea of goals, and they spend a lot of time fantasizing about the life they would like to live, but they don't engage with this energy. If you want things to happen, you need to participate in their creation. This card will let you know if you are more in love with the dream than you are with making it happen.

Use your journal to take notes about the cards in the spread. Keep in mind that these cards represent areas in your life that just need more love and attention. Really, all energy healing is designed to bring more love, compassion, and kindness to areas of our lives we normally beat ourselves up over.

Once you have worked your spread as much as you feel is possible, it is time to intuitively select your engagement significator. Some recommended cards are the Ten of Cups, the Seven of Wands, the Eight of Pentacles, the Lovers, the King of Pentacles, the Star, the Queen of Wands, the Three of Pentacles, and the Three of Cups. This card is a representation of how you want to engage in your life, such as the person you will become once you have activated that extra 10 percent on your engagement meter. Take this card to your journal and write about how your life will be when you allow the energy of this card into your daily world. Life can change quickly when we decide to participate more fully. Engaging just 10 percent more could change your life in ways you never thought possible.

. . . . .

## 6. Rebellion

They say everyone has a little rebel in them, and as it turns out, it is true, because the third chakra is our center of rebellion. Considering this is also the seat of our inner child, this isn't surprising. Some acts of so-called rebellion are nothing short of long, drawn-out temper tantrums. True rebellion works for a common cause, and it serves the betterment of all. Human stories, both myth and historical, are filled with acts of rebellion as a form of liberation, freedom, and revolution. Moses was a rebel, Gandhi was a rebel, and Nelson Mandela was a rebel. The entire Star Wars franchise is based on the act of political rebellion for the sake of unity and peace. Rebellion is in your blood, energetically anyway, yet not all acts of rebellion will be large, and not all of them have to be.

Most of us rebel in the smallest of ways each and every day. These small acts allow us to engage in the world on our own terms and to express ourselves in a way that we feel doesn't cause harm to ourselves and others. The more rules we have to abide by, the more rebellious we will become, as there are some things the soul self, which is the small part of us that ends up in our physical vessel and the self that is still connected to its divine self, cannot tolerate. Cruelty, injustice, restriction, limitation, oppression, suppression, and lack of freedom are just some of the things your rebel self was born to rise up against, and one of the most rebellious acts you do is to become one, yet again, with your divine self. Spirituality, not religion, is a rebel cause.

The path to the divine self is different for everyone, just as your act of rebellion will be different from others'. Perhaps religion plays a part in it, and perhaps it does not. Just know religion in and of itself is not necessary to being spiritual. The current Dalai Lama says that his spirituality is kindness, even though he is a Buddhist. His writings can teach us a lot about the act of rebellion, just not the type you think of when the word *rebel* first comes to mind. Brené Brown teaches acts of rebellion in her book *Rising Strong as a Spiritual Practice*. Byron Katie teaches acts of rebellion in her book *A Mind at Home with Itself* when she asks us to drop the dream and see beyond that which separates us from the truth. I am sure you have your own favorite spiritual rebel, and there is no doubt that their teachings have fed, nourished, and helped grow your inner rebel. Your teachers have lit a fire inside you, one that grows every time you brush up against something that goes against your spiritual core.

## EXERCISE
· · · · ·

As we work to bring your rebel self forth and speak openly about acts of rebellion, we also need to align this rebel self with a significator. For this exercise, we are going to use the major arcana only, so separate them from your deck. This card is to be chosen intuitively, not deliberately, which means you will keep your cards face down, give them a shuffle, and then select your card without looking at the images or knowing what card you will be selecting. You can select your card with your fingers, with a pendulum, or by splitting or cutting the deck. The act of selection itself is not as important as the intuitive part of allowing the card to speak to you. Pick up your major arcana cards and let your inner rebel answer the call. Once you have selected your card, open your journal and write at the top of a clean page "I *am* a rebellious_____ (whatever the name of your card is)" and the attributes that go along with the card that resonate with rebellion. Everything you think you know about this card now needs to be viewed through the lens of rebellion.

For example, let's say you've chosen the Tower. "I am a rebellious Tower" is your starting point. When viewing the Tower through the lens of rebellion, we can see how shaking things up and pulling old ways of thinking down to create more inclusive thinking is the path of the rebel. Maybe you got the Temperance card; therefore, your statement would read, "I am a rebellious Temperance," and this card is about alchemy and healing. I often think of people who create healing essential oil blends, herbalists creating healing tinctures, or even energy workers when Temperance shows up in a reading, because the act of creating something that is outside of big pharmaceuticals becomes an act of rebellion. Working with the natural world in order to find the balance of health and healing is very much a rebellious act these days.

Once you have made a list of the ways your card rebels, think about how these acts relate to you. How do you align with the rebellion energy of this card? Start making notes about when, where or how this energy has shown up in your life in the past and where you actively and willingly engaged with it in a proactive way. This might take you some time, so do not rush it. If, however, you are struggling to connect with the card you selected or you can't seem to find examples of using this energy in the past, understand that this is a new energy for you. This is the rebel that you are becoming, one that is asking for you to acknowledge it. Use this time to get to know your card and allow it to introduce itself. You may feel more comfortable taking this card to your meditation cushion, sitting with it, and holding sacred space together. If this is the case, just place the card where you can see it and keep your gaze focused on it as you settle into your breath work. As you breathe and gaze at the card, imagine yellow light coming up from your solar plexus and out through your breath. See it as it forms a protective bubble around you and your card. Relax as best you can and keep focusing on your card. Just allow whatever bubbles up to rise. Do not try to hold on to it; just let the mind flow. Sit in this space for as long as necessary, and when you are done, pick your journal back up and write down your thoughts or feelings.

How you connect with your rebel card will be as unique as your own rebellious energy, which means there is no wrong or right way to work with our new significator. The important thing is to work with it and allow it to help you heal and clear your third chakra.

$\cdot$ $\cdot$ $\cdot$ $\cdot$

## 7. Action

There is no doubting there is a lot of action in the third chakra, as it is full of fire and movement, but this is also our "act or react" chakra, as well as our "move forward and do it" or "procrastinate and freeze" chakra. Whenever we decide to act or not act, that decision is made here. Hyperactive behavior can be caused by an overactive solar plexus, just as people who suffer from sluggish behavior may have a slow and unhealthy solar plexus. In other words, this energy center has the ability to either speed us up, slow us down, move us from one task to another, or cause us fear and paralysis. If you are ever looking for both the cause and the solution to your procrastination, look no further than the solar plexus. Books like *The 5 Second Rule* have become so popular because they tap straight into your center of action. Mel Robbins's formula is ingeniously simple: count down from five and move.[6] It is one of the most direct ways to engage your solar plexus, get your energy out of fear, and shift yourself into a space of action.

Obviously, we don't need to act on every little thing. Sometimes doing nothing is the best action we can take, but think about all the experiences you didn't have because you never acted on them. Think about how you felt fear and doubt and allowed them to turn your feet into concrete, while your stomach tied itself up in knots panicking over the repercussions of doing something you felt drawn to do. We have all done it. We have all worked ourselves into a tizzy while we engaged in stress, directing it straight to our stomachs and liver. The more stress, the higher our acid levels become, and this in turn can have an unhealthy impact on the internal workings of our body. However, all of this could be prevented by following the simple five-second rule Mel Robbins teaches in her book, so count down from five, engage positive energy through the solar plexus, and move!

## EXERCISE
· · · · ·

Because of all the constant flip-flopping and jumping around this energy center does, it makes pulling a significator card interesting. This card will need to work in its upright aspect as well as its reversed. You are looking for a card that you want to represent both the positive, easy-flowing movement of action and the procrastination energy that can be brought about by second-guessing

---

6. Mel Robbins, *The 5 Second Rule: Transform Your Life, Work, and Confidence with Everyday Courage* (self-published, Savio Republic, 2017).

yourself. This means you will want to choose this card deliberately, so get your cards out and start looking for a good image to start with. Recommended cards may be the Chariot, the Knight of Swords, the Knight of Wands, the Eight of Wands, the Six of Swords, the Tower, the Fool, the Devil, and even the World.

Once you have your card selected, it's time to create two mantras or affirmation statements for this card: one for when this card is in power, meaning when it is upright and flowing, and one for when it is blocked. Let's say you choose the Knight of Swords as your significator card. Your mantras or affirmations might be something like these:

- *In power, I ride toward what I want, cutting away all thoughts of fear and doubt.*
- *When I am blocked, I run around in circles unable to find a clear path to ride upon.*

Maybe you went for the Six of Swords, and your affirmations might be like these:

- *In power, I know when to confidently move from one situation to another with ease and grace.*
- *When I am blocked, putting distance between myself and things that no longer serve me makes me feel marooned, like a boat with no sail or oar.*

Now at this point you might very well be asking why you should write up negative affirmations. First of all, they aren't negative, and second, being able to assess how you are feeling and where you currently are is the first step to action. When you speak your blocked mantra or affirmation out loud, it will shift energy inside your solar plexus. More than likely you won't feel totally aligned to it and will be more inclined to move out of the funk, but even if you don't, being able to just sit and see the energy as an observer, detached from the outcome, is incredibly healing. Sitting with your blocked affirmation in mediation could very quickly turn that energy around. It is only when we try to deny this shadow self and ignore our emotions that we end up getting stuck.

Now let's take this significator card and see how it affects the rest of your chakra energy. Do this chakra pillar twice and keep a picture of it. You want to do it once with your action significator in the upright aspect and once with it in the reversed aspect, as it is going to change the energy that is running up and down your chakras. This is similar to the one you did at the very beginning of this book, but for this chakra pillar, we are using all different cards for a totally different reading. You can see that the first three cards are already assigned with significator cards from the previous chapters. When you reverse your action card and redo this spread, make sure to reverse the root and sacral as well, as this will give you a much clearer picture of what your energy looks like when you are panicking, fearful, and full of doubt. Cards 4, 5, 6, and 7 you will draw intuitively from your deck, and you can shuffle and select the remaining four cards anyway you choose, as long as you do it with the cards face down.

- *Card 7:* Crown Chakra
- *Card 6:* Third Eye Chakra
- *Card 5:* Throat Chakra
- *Card 4:* Heart Chakra
- *Card 3:* Solar Plexus Chakra Action Significator, Upright and Reversed
- *Card 2:* Sacral Chakra Pleasure Significator
- *Card 1:* Root Chakra Safety Significator

This spread is going to give you a lot of information that may take you a couple of days to work through, especially considering you are doing this spread twice. It might be useful to map this spread out in your journal and see each chakra as a single destination on a longer journey, with the first stop being the root and the last stop and final destination being the crown. What energy and experiences do you gather on your trip, and how is it affecting the overall experience of your journey? Also, consider doing a compare and contrast report on the two versions of the spread. Think of this like two similar products you are reviewing. Neither is good or bad; they just have subtle differences. Again, this sort of exercise puts you in the seat of the observer, removing your ego mind and releasing your emotional triggers. The important thing is to take as much time as you need with these two spreads. Collect as much information as you can and use it as part of the healing energy you're building and sending to your solar plexus.

· · · · ·

## Solar Plexus Chakra Tarot Healing

Now that you have worked through the seven key issues of the third chakra, it is time to do some energy healing work on all that you have discovered, all that has bubbled up, and all that has presented itself for cleaning and clearing. Grab your tarot deck and get out the significator cards for the issues covered in this chapter. Select your significator card for the solar plexus and place it in front of you. This card is going to be the middle card in your solar plexus wheel.

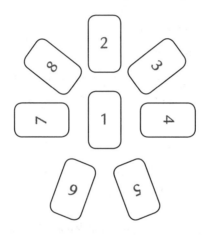

Your card order is as follows:

- *Card 1:* Solar Plexus Chakra Significator
- *Card 2:* Self-Expression Significator
- *Card 3:* Empowerment Significator
- *Card 4:* Worthiness Significator
- *Card 5:* Play Significator
- *Card 6:* Engagement Significator
- *Card 7:* Rebellion Significator
- *Card 8:* Action Significator

Your center card is going to be the energy you will see flowing in and out of the other cards, as if a beautiful yellow smoke wisps out of the card and starts to tickle the other cards around it. As we move into the visualization part of this exercise, move your hands over the cards as you say the following affirmations for each of the cards surrounding your solar plexus significator. The tarot mandala helps anchor your energy healing work and allows you to engage more fully with the overall process. Your affirmations are as follows:

- *Card 2:* I am confident with who and what I am.
- *Card 3:* I am strong and capable.
- *Card 4:* I am enough. I always have been and always will be.
- *Card 5:* I am a playful child in the playground of a loving universe.
- *Card 6:* I am engaging in all areas of my life.
- *Card 7:* I am embracing my rebellious nature.
- *Card 8:* I am inspiration in action.

Find somewhere comfortable and quiet, where you won't be disturbed for up to twenty minutes. Place your cards where you can see them and start rubbing your palms gently together as you focus on your breathing. Rub your hands together for about forty seconds, activating the energy centers in your palms. You might start to feel some heat in your hands, and this is good. Now place your hands above your belly button and focus on your breath, inhaling through your nose. Feel the breath as it hits the back of your throat, fills your lungs, and expands your belly. As you exhale from the mouth, feel the breath leaving your body and notice the depression of the abdomen. Let the breath work become automatic and shift your focus to your cards, starting with the center card, which is your solar plexus significator. Visualize the yellow smoke gently rising from the card and twirling around the wheel you have created around it. Each time you exhale, the smoky wisps extend farther and farther. Sit like this for a few minutes, just doing the breath work and keeping your hands on your stomach as you feel it rise and fall, and visualize the smoky orange energy infusing your spread.

When you feel ready, move your hands to your tarot mandala and move them along each card as you speak the corresponding affirmation statements out loud. Read through the entire list three times. Once you have finished, just relax and focus on the breath work, placing the hands back over the solar plexus. As you inhale, feel the smoky yellow energy coming into your nose, hitting the back of your throat, filling up your lungs and moving into your solar plexus under your hands. Relax into this, as you inhale all of this lovely infused energy, and let this energy clean and clear your solar plexus, as it embeds your affirmations into your chakra. When this feels complete, remove your hands and just breathe normally for thirty to forty seconds. Thank your cards, and you are done.

You can repeat this simple tarot healing session anytime you want, and by all means, journal about how the session made you feel or any revelations you had during the session. The more you know, the more you inquire, the more you heal.

# The Heart Chakra

Welcome to the heart of your energy system—literally. The heart chakra is the midway point through your chakra system and, because of this, tends to act as a mediator between the lower earth chakras and the higher ethereal chakras. This chakra sits in the center of your chest and affects your heart, lungs, and breasts. Obviously, we need our heart, as it basically keeps us upright and tethered to our body. It's also pretty difficult to breathe without lungs, even though for an asthmatic like me, it can be difficult to breathe with them. I know what it's like when your lungs aren't doing their best work, but they are vital nonetheless. Last, both men and women are susceptible to breast cancer, yet another reason to give attention to our vital heart chakra. Inside this chapter, you are going to explore seven issues the heart chakra deals with on a consistent and ongoing basis. These seven issues each have their own section in this chapter, as they all have important information for you regarding the health and well-being of your heart chakra.

The sections are as follows:

1. Fellowship

2. Love

3. Empathy

4. Compassion

5. Forgiveness

6. Kindness

7. Gratitude

## Anahata

While the sacral chakra is the emotional center of your chakra system, the heart chakra, also known as *anahata*, is the feeling center of it. Through ongoing research from the HeartMath foundation, we know that "the heart actually sends more signals to the brain than the brain sends to the heart."[7] This makes the heart center our first brain, our feeling brain, which means we process the majority of the information that comes our way via feeling. What we feel about something affects how the rest of the chakra system reacts to it. This makes the heart chakra the center of mission control for our entire energetic body. It is important to point out here that feelings are not emotions, as they have no embedded memory and no ingrained trigger to them. You can feel something without ever having experienced it before. This may seem like a subtle difference between feelings and emotions, but it is an important one, especially considering that the heart is constantly talking to the other chakras and is always pulling information up or down to create a complete picture of how the body and mind should or should not be acting or reacting in any given moment. The heart chakra needs

---

7. "The Science of HeartMath," HeartMath, accessed January 15, 2020, https://www.heartmath.com/science.

to filter all sorts of information and make sure that it responds in a way that serves your overall health and well-being.

The heart chakra is sensitive and empathic, while also being resilient and strong. Because we are feeling beings, our heart is an echo chamber for any pain and suffering we see outside of ourselves as well as any goodness and compassion. Random acts of kindness can light us up and expand us, just as hearing about another mass shooting can tighten us up and make us contract. The heart filters a world that is split into two, so it is constantly working with duality, and in order to find a way through this split world, it has devised its own language. The language of the heart is a simple one. What you send out you get back, because for the heart, there is no you and there is no world. There is only energy that goes out and energy that goes in. Send out love, compassion, and kindness, and see oneness, love, compassion, and kindness come back to you. Send out fear, hate, and anger while focusing on separation and fear, then hate and anger will come back to you. It is a simple and elegant communication system with no room for confusion or misinterpretation. Whatever feeling you send out through your heart chakra is the feeling that comes back in through your heart chakra. This means we are not communicating with the vastness of our universe with our minds, but rather we are doing it with our hearts. People spend a lot of time concerned about their thoughts when really they should be more focused on the messages being transmitted by their heart. The language of the heart dictates the language of the mind, so let's explore what your heart is saying.

## EXERCISE
· · · · ·
What message is your heart chakra beaming out into the world each and every second of the day and night,

and is it the type of message you really want to be transmitting? The answer to this question is the card you will select as your heart chakra significator. Grab your deck and place it face up so you can see the cards. You will need to be able to see this card in order to connect a feeling to it. Think about what sort of energy you want to start focusing on in your heart, as this is the energy that will affect all your lower and higher chakras, and this card will be the language with which your heart will engage. Before you select your card for this chakra, take a moment to just connect with your heart chakra.

With your deck spread out in front of you, place both hands over your heart, right hand on top, and take a nice, deep breath. Settle yourself into your heart space as you take another breath, and apply a small amount of pressure to your heart chakra area. Gently press the hands into the chest, and feel the breath as it moves in and out of your lungs. Close your eyes for a moment, and just surrender to this breath-heart connection. Now remove your hands, taking another nice long and deep breath, and select your card. Some recommended cards are the Star, the Six of Pentacles, the Ace of Wands, the Ace of Cups, the Hierophant, Strength, Temperance, the Queen of Cups, and the Four of Wands. When you select your card, take it to your journal and write about how you feel with this energy in your heart and how you see this card communicating out into the world and bringing energy back.

I recommend seeing if you can also come up with a list of words that this card might speak through your heart. If these are words you are used to speaking on a daily basis, make it a practice to start incorporating them. For example, the words for the Star might be *wishes, dreams, true north, travel, journeys in the dark,* and *direction.* If some of these words are not in your normal day-to-day experience, think about spending more time talking about your dreams and wishes and finding ways to take more journeys. This card is teaching you a new language, a new way of communicating that perhaps you have not considered before. Let this card guide you through a new way of seeing, exploring, and creating a truly heart-centered world.

• • • • •

## 1. Fellowship

The heart likes to be around beings who have similar vibes. It will actively seek these beings out in many varied ways. This is not because it needs to belong somewhere but because it understands that there is no separation between itself and others. This is why most of us do better when we feel a sense of community, camaraderie, or fellowship. This could be the reason one of the catchphrases of the early twenty-first century has been "Find your tribe." However, here in the heart, we seek these experiences to keep us in a specific vibrational state, not because we feel alone, left out, or alienated. This is a very important distinction to make. Fellowship itself does not necessarily mean friendly, nor does it mean you will be treated with open arms. Fellowship is a space where people come together for a common cause, a common experience, and a common sense of overall well-being. This could be done with one person or with one hundred people. There are no real hard-and-fast rules for how your heart will find fellowship. Conferences, conventions, expos, and festivals are places of fellowship. Offices, workspaces, board meetings, and Skype meetings are all spaces for fellowship. Churches, reiki circles, drumming circles, and meditation or yoga class are all places for fellowship. Hiking groups, sports clubs, and outdoor adventure clubs are also places for fellowship. Bookstores, author events, and book clubs are places for fellowship. I think you are starting to get the picture. Right now in your life, your heart has somewhere it goes for fellowship. You may not have connected the dots until now, but that is your heart chakra making sure it is around a vibration and energy it needs in order to assist you with optimal health and well-being. How smart your heart is!

So where do you go for fellowship?

Who are your people, and how do they make you feel?

Confession time. Until I started writing this section, I had not thought too hard about this aspect of the heart chakra. I had not really explored how the heart has its own call and seeks out its own likeness. I knew it on a theoretical level, but I hadn't really thought about it seriously on a practical level. It has made me stop and pay closer attention to how my heart is connecting me to people, places, and things. It seems the heart bypasses the mind when it comes to fellowship. It is not so much interested in what the mind thinks we should be doing, based on the information the brain processes. No, the heart works with the deeper energy in all seven chakras to find us fellowship that will align us, balance us, and restore the chakra system. It does all this, without us even knowing about it, by sending out vibrational pulses, constantly matching us up with similar pulses, and guiding us into experiences that have the ability to heal us and keep us alive. That is quite extraordinary.

## EXERCISE

· · · · ·

Let's take this another step and give your center for fellowship a significator. Recommended cards here are the Lovers, the Two of Cups, the Four of Wands, the Ten of Cups, the Ten of Pentacles, the World, and the Seven of Wands. I recommend you select this card intuitively, as it would give you the most accurate reading of how your center for fellowship is working, but you do not have to. Instead, you may wish to find a card that best aligns to how you want to see fellowship play out in your day-to-day experience, and that is perfectly fine. Once you have selected your card, take it to your journal and spend some time with it. Think about how this card is talking to your heart chakra, and see if you can write up a dialogue between them. See if you can let yourself imagine what a conversation between your heart chakra and this card would be like and what sort of topics these two like to talk about. There is obviously no wrong or right way to do this; just allow yourself to imagine and write.

Once you have done your journal work, place your significator card in front of you and find the connection significator card from the root chakra, the engagement card from the solar plexus chakra, and the pleasure significator card from the sacral chakra. Lay them out in the following spread:

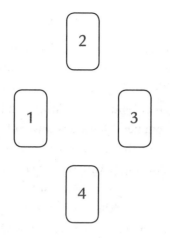

- *Card 1:* Fellowship Significator
- *Card 2:* Connection Significator
- *Card 3:* Engagement Significator
- *Card 4:* Pleasure Significator

Here you will see how your heart is allowing you to connect, engage, and find pleasure in the realm of fellowship. This gives you a very visual picture of how your heart chakra gathers its intel and then sends you off on secret missions to find other beings with like vibes. With this spread, you can see all the communication between the chakras in living color, and it is fascinating to behold. So now that you are looking at these cards, is this conversation one you would have expected or is this all new information to you? Work with this spread in your journal and do the dialogue exercise with these cards, just like we did above with the fellowship significator card. Imagine how these cards are constantly chatting with one another. Think about the personalities behind the voices. See if you can imagine which cards are the serious ones and which ones are the cheeky ones. If you feel creatively inclined, you could even put these cards and their dialogue into a short story. Perhaps it could be a story of four friends conspiring to get a mutual friend (that would be you) back out into the world again. Place this conversation in a setting, like a coffee shop or at a sporting event. Get as involved with this story as you want. Just let your imagination play and see what bubbles out of you and onto the page. In other words, have fun, play, and let the energy of your heart chakra flow through you and into your journal.

· · · · ·

## 2. Love

Welcome to the most misunderstood issue and concept in humanity. I know that's a bold statement—just bear with me. Love for the heart chakra is not the love you probably think about. This is an energy, a pure one, and an energy that doesn't know good from bad but only how to give and receive. It does not judge, it does not question, and it has no condition of expectations. It asks for nothing and expects nothing in return. This is divine love, the love that flows in and out of your heart chakra day in and day out without you even knowing about it. The only time this love has problems is when you try to dictate who or what it should or should not flow to.

When we try to dictate the energy of love, things can, and do, go horribly wrong. If you have ever read or seen *How the Grinch Stole Christmas!*, you know what I am talking about. That story showed us the innocence of love, how it is not something we have any control over, and how it affects one's heart and, ultimately, one's view of themselves and the world in general. When we try to control the natural state of our heart chakra, we become closed off, suspicious, and bitter, and we may become susceptible to chest infections, breast issues, and heart problems. Closing off or strangling the natural flow of love from the heart center basically turns your fourth chakra into a backup second chakra. You push your emotions into your heart and start making emotion-based decisions. The heart is not an emotional center, and this is very important to understand. It is a feeling chakra, and it allows feelings to pump in, out, and around without any need to attach meaning, context, or judgment to them. Your fourth chakra should never function as a backup second chakra, yet unfortunately, that is exactly the way many people are running this particular chakra energy.

When I used to see reiki clients on a regular basis, I would see how they had pushed energy from the sacral into the heart all the time. When my wife got her aura camera, in a photo we had taken we could clearly see orange, reds, and yellows around the heart center instead of greens or pinks. I still believe it is because we keep trying to mold the energy of love into a conditional, emotional experience.

## EXERCISE
· · · · ·

Now this begs the question, what does heart chakra love look like to you?

It is time to find a significator for this energy. Recommended cards are the Ace of Cups, the Six of Pentacles, Three of Swords, Eight of Wands, Strength, the Hanged Man, Temperance, and the Empress. You may see that I have placed the Three of Swords in this lineup.

I believe it is a fantastic card to show the energy of love because, like heart chakra love, the Three of Swords is a very misunderstood card. It is, however, not for everyone, and it might be a hard energy for you to work with, so be mindful of that as you move through the cards to find the right one for your significator. You will select this card deliberately and intentionally, so spread your cards out and find your love card. Once you have your card selected, take it to your journal and discuss how this will benefit your life and what challenges it may present as you move out of emotional conditions into a judgment-free relationship with love.

It is important to understand that this particular function of the heart chakra is not an easy one, because we are not trained or conditioned to love everything and everyone in our lives. We are taught to hide our hearts, to save them for someone special, to set boundaries around our love, and to never freely give of ourselves in any way. We are strongly programmed to expect something in return for our love and told that if we do not get it, then we are being used, and this person is not worthy of what we give them freely. It is not easy to admit that love doesn't turn on and off like a tap, but rather it just flows all the time, without us doing anything. Our interference, our mind, and our emotional throttle block and try to stem this flow, which in turn causes us pain, suffering, and sometimes disease. Our misconceptions of what love as an energy is can possibly harm us.

Once you have journaled with your card and you feel you have nothing else to discuss at this time, place it in front of you face up. Pick up the rest of your deck and just hold the cards for a moment. Take a couple of nice, deep breaths and imagine a beautiful green or pink light radiating out of your chest moving down your arms and into your cards. As this light surrounds your cards, begin to shuffle them slowly, asking, "What does love want me to know today?" Shuffle until you feel you are done, the cards are infused, and your question has been answered. Now cut the deck, take the top card, and place it face up on top of your significator card. This is a direct message from your heart chakra, so read it carefully. If you need more clarification, repeat the process again and add another card or two. I do not recommend more than three cards and highly recommend you stick with just one. Take your card or cards to your journal and ponder the following questions:

- What message does love have for me today?
- Where can I apply this message in my life right now?
- How had I been resisting this message in the past?

As you answer these questions, you will more than likely go deeper and collect even more information for the heart to use later. This is good, and to be encouraged, so keep asking, keep exploring, and keep the heart chakra love flowing.

• • • • •

## 3. Empathy

True empathy almost feels like an impossible thing. "Walk a mile in someone else's shoes," the saying goes, but can we really ever do that? Empathy is the ability to understand other people's feelings. In most spiritual teachings, empathy is about being able to identify someone else's behavior in yourself, allowing you to see that empathy acknowledges no separation from the outside world with the inside world of self. All of these give different ways to approach empathy, yet all of them require a pretty large shift in the way we perceive ourselves and the world of our creation. It is a shift that we have not all been taught or equipped with. Empathy is one of those things that sound good on paper and seems like a kind and decent thing to aspire to have. I am sure most of us think we do act with empathy when the need arises. However, the more I learn about the heart chakra, the more I question if we really understand empathy at all.

Empathy practiced through the mind is an exercise in trying to understand something about someone that we perceive as different and acknowledge that we are walking different paths, making different choices, and creating different karma and consequences. Empathy via the heart, however, asks us to view everything as ourselves, with no separation. The battle between the mind and heart is where we fail to enter into a true state of empathy, for as long as we view it as something that is asking us to see the world through the eyes of someone different to us, we are not in the vibration of empathy at all. Perhaps this means the saying becomes "Can you walk a mile in your own shoes as a refugee, a homeless person, a murderer, a cheat, a thief, or someone else you previously thought was different from you?"

*Ho'oponopono*, a Hawaiian practice of forgiveness, was adapted and popularized in the early 2000s by Joe Vitale and Dr. Ihaleakala Hew Len as a problem-solving method. Vitale and Len illustrate this form of heart chakra empathy beautifully. In the book *Zero Limits*, they discuss how Len cured an entire ward of certified mentally unstable patients, to the point where they had to close the ward down.[8] He did this by doing nothing but "cleaning" himself, or to put it another way, using empathy so he could see himself as all the other patients.[9] Len also never saw any of these patients in person; he just read their files and asked the question "What is it in me I see in these patients?" and started the ho'oponopono process. This process is four short sentences:

> *I'm sorry.*
> *Please forgive me.*
> *I love you.*
> *Thank you.*[10]

These are the words of a heart filled with empathy.

## EXERCISE
· · · · ·

Using these four simple statements, you are going to select your empathy significator. Pick up your deck and hold it close to your heart, repeat the ho'oponopono lines three times, take a nice, deep breath, and then fan the cards out in front of you face down and select your card. If you have not drawn this card in the reserved aspect, please flip it and make it so. What is

8. Ihaleakala Hew Len and Joe Vitale, *Zero Limits: The Secret Hawaiian System for Health, Wealth, Peace, and More* (Hoboken, NJ: Wiley, 2007), chapter 2.

9. Len and Vitale, *Zero Limits,* 31–32.

10. Len and Vitale, *Zero Limits,* 32.

slightly different about this card compared to some of the significators you have selected thus far is this card is showing you a version of yourself that is coming up for what Dr. Len calls "cleaning." This is the self that you are seeing reflected in the world around you that is begging for true heart chakra empathy. This card will show up in people around you and, by doing so, remind you that this version of yourself still needs healing, understanding, and love. Take this card to your journal and write on this version of yourself for as long as you feel you can, making all sorts of notes on personality traits, behavioral patterns, social etiquette, and the like. See if you can create a profile on this version of yourself, because this is really you putting your feet in the shoes of someone you are now seeing as not separate from yourself.

When you feel you have written all you can for one sitting, place your card on an altar, on top of a bookcase, or somewhere you can see it as you sit in front of it. Set a timer on your phone for two minutes. Light a candle, burn some sage or palo santo, and take some nice cleansing breaths. Hit the timer and, while looking at your card, say the ho'oponopono statements out loud, and keep doing so until your timer beeps to let you know the two minutes are up. If possible, leave the candle burning for some time. However, if you are going to be leaving the house, by all means blow it out, and make sure you have nothing else left burning on your altar.

If you have time, take your card back to your journal and write with it again. See if doing some of the empathy work on it has shifted the way you view it or consider it. If you don't have time to do the journal work right after doing the hoʻoponopono, then consider planning a time when you can do the exercise again and allow at least twenty minutes for journaling afterward.

You can do this exercise with your card as often as you feel called to. Each time you do it, make sure you do the journal work so you can document any shifts in energy or perceptions you are having. As you continue to work with empathy, you will also work on the lower chakras as well, so be mindful of things bubbling up from below that will be connected or tethered to the card or issue that is the focus of your empathy work.

Empathy in and of itself may still be a strange and impossible thing, but at least now you have a tool to assist you with connecting to the heart energy that it truly is.

• • • • •

## 4. Compassion

Unlike empathy, compassion doesn't require you to identify with a person or situation to connect with it on a feeling level. You can be compassionate without understanding the experience another sentient being is going through. Compassion means you have chosen to not make that suffering any worse. Compassion is something that comes easily and naturally to us, even though in our dog-eat-dog world it seems compassion is becoming extinct. It can seem hard to come up with examples of compassion in our day-to-day lives, mainly because we tend not to be very compassionate with ourselves. Sometimes it feels like our hearts have been hardened to the suffering of the world, because it just feels like there is too much to bear. The media flashes us with pictures of war, famine, mass shootings, and aggression on a pretty consistent basis. Not that these are not important social issues, but the constant stream of bad news can overwhelm us. It can harden us and make us feel like we need to withdraw from our communities for our own emotional protection. It can make being compassionate feel like a chore, something we don't always have the energy to participate in. However, compassion is an essential part of heart chakra energy. We need it to keep the energy center open, flowing, and healthy, which means it is important to have compassion working at some level of your life.

## EXERCISE
· · · · ·

In this exercise, you will find your compassion significator and then move it into a compassion spread. Your compassion significator will represent what compassion means to you. Look closely at the images for this card and don't focus too much on the card name or the meaning of the card. Instead, allow yourself to be drawn to the visual image. It should move you in some way and stir feelings around the heart center. Recommended cards to look at in your decks might be Strength, the Star, the Ace of Cups, the Empress, the Hanged Man, the Devil reversed, Temperance, the Six of Pentacles, and the Five of Pentacles reversed.

Once you have your card selected, place it face up in front of you. Pick up your deck and hold it to your heart chakra. Take a couple of nice, deep breaths, and as you do, imagine a beautiful pink light coming out of your chest and into your cards. See this light weave its way around your deck, infusing your cards with compassion energy straight from your heart. Now begin to shuffle slowly, just focusing on the connection you have to your heart space and the cards. When you feel the deck has been shuffled enough, you are going to draw four cards and lay them around your compassion significator like so:

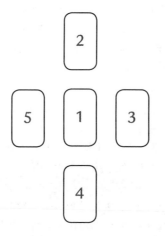

- *Card 1:* Your compassion significator.
- *Card 2:* Your compassion energy flowing to your immediate family.
- *Card 3:* Your compassion energy flowing to your work colleagues or employees.
- *Card 4:* Your compassion energy flowing to pets, animals, or the animal kingdom in general.
- *Card 5:* Your compassion energy flowing to your houseplants, garden, trees, or the natural world in general.

This spread is not meant to make you feel bad about yourself in any way. It is merely to show you where you feel safe opening your heart and where you do not. If you see cards that make you feel sad, despondent, or uncomfortable, just know that these are areas of your heart that are stepping forth for healing. Honor them not by trying to select another "better" card, but instead see them, thank them, and let them know that you are open to showering them with more compassion in the future. Take these cards to your journal and write about what you see. Explore these parts of your life that you don't seem to have a good compassion connection with, and just allow yourself to observe why this might be without the need to judge or fix it.

The trick with heart chakra healing work is to understand that sometimes we don't always feel safe to open our hearts because we have wounds that live in our heart chakra. This is perfectly okay and normal, and it is one of the reasons you are reading this book and doing your healing work. You are finding the parts of yourself that need the most love, compassion, kindness, and attention. If, perhaps, finding compassion for yourself or humanity is just too much for you right now, then start with an animal, a plant, a flower, or even a tree, especially if they end up with cards that show a nice compassion connection. That is really what this spread is doing, showing you where you are streaming compassion and where it is streaming back.

So what is it? Once you have identified it in your spread, shower it with compassion every single day and allow yourself to receive compassion back from it, because you will. Letting another living being shower you with compassion can be the first step in allowing yourself to be gentler with yourself and to heal some of those heart wounds you are still carrying. Just set an intention to slowly and gently open the heart chakra back up to compassion.

• • • • •

## 5. Forgiveness

Forgiveness is probably one of the more complex issues we deal with here in the heart chakra, mainly because there are so many schools of thought on what forgiveness is and how one forgives. It would seem everyone has an idea about how you forgive, who you forgive, and why you forgive. I have to admit, none of them were very compelling to me for the longest time. As a survivor of domestic violence, I was always being told that in order to move on with my life, I had to forgive and let go. This felt impossible to do. To forgive the person who intentionally and strategically hurt me over and over again, to see the person who enjoyed inflicting pain upon me free and clear of their sins, seemed such a wrong thing to ask of anyone. The greater the pain, the harder forgiveness becomes, which is why I am not going to tell you how you should personally form a relationship with forgiveness. It is much too intimate. Instead, I shall show you how I came to a place of peace with it and how I have taught it to my clients.

For me, forgiveness is about forgiving yourself. That is how I have been able to use forgiveness as an act of healing and an act of self-love and compassion. When I was coming to terms with the dark and horrific elements of my abuse, I slowly but surely started to forgive myself. I had to dig deep into forgiving the person I used to be, the person who allowed such things to be done to them, the person who thought there was no way out, the person who gave up their power, and the version of myself that I never, ever wanted to be again. That was where I directed my forgiveness. I had to stand in the shoes of the person I now am and send that forgiveness, kindness, and compassion to the person I used to be, even though it is difficult to see that version of myself, the version I pushed away into the shadows, because she was broken, weak, and unacceptable.

This act of forgiving myself has become a lifelong process, as there are so many layers to unpack. It has also become a lifelong process for some of my clients as well. My path to forgiveness may not be your path, and that is okay. Regardless of which path you choose to take, the following exercises will be helpful and show you just how well you are doing, and how much more work you have to do, with healing this part of your heart chakra energy.

## EXERCISE
· · · · ·

To begin or deepen your forgiveness work, you need to select a significator card. This card should show the energy of who you want to be as the person in the act and flow of forgiveness. Keep in mind that forgiveness is an energy. It flows through us, in us, and around us, so think about who or what makes you feel like you are being a vessel for this energy. Recommended cards are the High Priestess, the Hierophant, all the queens, Strength, Temperance, the Star, and of course Judgement, the ultimate card of self-forgiveness. Once you have selected your card, remembering you do not have to go with any of the ones I have recommended, take this card to your journal and explain why this card instills you with a feeling of forgiveness. Get into as much detail as possible. You have to be able to explain clearly how and why you see this card as a representation of someone who is good at forgiving, and why you want this card to assist you in your forgiveness healing journey. Take your time with your journal, and don't rush it.

Once you have finished with your journal writing, pick up your deck and remove the fives from it. Lay them out in front of you in a row in the following order: Five of Pentacles, Five of Swords, Five of Wands, and Five of Cups. Place your forgiveness significator card above this row of fives. Starting with the Five of Pentacles, say out loud, "I forgive myself for …" and then say whatever comes to mind. It might be something like "I forgive myself for not asking for help," "I forgive myself for making life harder than it needs to be," or "I forgive myself for keeping distance between myself and those who could bring me comfort."

When you feel you have nothing left to say, pick up the Five of Swords and say out loud, "I forgive myself for …" and again say whatever comes to mind. It could be something along the lines of "I forgive myself for needing to be right all the time," "I forgive myself for being bossy," "I forgive myself for always being on the defensive," or "I forgive myself for wanting things my way." Keep going until you run out of things to say.

Then move on to the Five of Wands and repeat the process. You might say things like "I forgive myself for always being reactive," "I forgive myself for needing to be combative," "I forgive myself for feeling angry all the time," or "I forgive myself for being hard on myself and others." Again, just keep going until you feel spent.

Now move on to the last card, the Five of Cups. Repeat this process one last time. Things that might come up are "I forgive myself for being a bit of an emotional mess," "I forgive myself for dwelling in the past," "I forgive myself for not being able to let things go," or "I forgive myself for constantly feeling overwhelmed." Again, just keep going until you have run out of things to say.

If you feel inclined, you might wish to head back to your journal and write about some of things that this exercise bought up, and if you need to have a good cry, do that as well. Crying is deeply healing, as it allows us to release blocked trauma.

Working with the energy of forgiveness is never easy and is always messy, so remember to be kind and compassionate to yourself as you finish up this section. I recommend going for a nice cleansing walk after you have completed the above exercise to clean out your aura, ground your energy back into your body, and allow your heart chakra to feel connected to the vibrations of the everyday world.

· · · · ·

## 6. Kindness

The Dalai Lama is constantly saying in his interviews and writing in his books that even though he is just a simple monk, his true religion is kindness. As a heart chakra warrior, his holiness believes kindness to be so important that we should make it a devotional practice. The idea of kindness as a form of devotion is very different from kindness as an act. It pushes us to embrace kindness as a way of life, as a philosophy, and not as something we do because it seems appropriate in the moment. For most people, kindness is something that is done for other people. We see it as a bit of a choice, such as you can either be an asshat or you can be kind. However, if we take on the Dalai Lama's devotional practice of kindness, there are no choices, and we just walk through the world as a beacon of kindness. In essence we would become kindness, much the way all spiritual devotees become a manifestation of their faith.

Like in all devotional practices, it would mean we have to start with ourselves first, and this is where the majority of us trip up. It is always easier to project out of ourselves than it is to be present and internally focused. It is interesting that gratitude journals have become such a big deal over the past few years but not kindness journals. Imagine how different your life would be if you recorded how many times a day you were kind to yourself. Contemplate for a second how your day would flow if you started it by opening up your heart chakra and automatically went into kindness devotion the moment you rolled out of bed. Think about how differently your internal script would be if the first thing you did each day was not check the news, not check your phone, not think about all the things that cause you stress, but instead do something kind for yourself and thought about how you would spread that spark of kindness throughout the rest of your day. Devotional practices are nothing more than perception filters, and they let us view ourselves and everything around us based on that practice. I can't speak for you, but I for one am all for the Dalai Lama's new religion of kindness and will gladly pick up this new lens to view the world and my place in it.

## EXERCISE
· · · · ·

The first step in being a heart chakra kindness warrior is to deliberately and intentionally pick your significator card. This card should represent either how you see yourself as a kindness warrior or how you would like to see yourself, a version of you that you are committed to growing into. Card recommendations for this are the Knight, Queen, and King of Cups; Strength; the Seven of Wands; the Three of Pentacles; the Knight, Queen, and King of Pentacles; the Emperor; the Empress; Justice; Judgement; Temperance; and the World. Make sure you select a card that you feel some sort of connection with on a heart chakra level, as this is the energy center the card works with.

Once you have your card, hold it up to your heart chakra and take a few deep breaths while you make a deeper connection to the card itself. Now take it to your journal and write about how you see yourself as this card, either in the present moment or in the future. Imagine yourself and the image becoming one. Feel the clothes they are wearing, and notice how they fit on you. Allow their heart chakra, kindness, and devotee energy to fill you, and write about how it feels to have that much kindness pumping through your body. Take as much time as you need with this journal work. There is no need to rush on to the next part of this exercise.

When you feel you have written as much as you can with your card, pick up your deck, leaving your significator out and facing you, and hold the deck to your heart chakra. Take a few nice, deep breaths, and imagine pink and gold light coming out of your heart and enveloping the deck in your hands. See this light infusing the deck and filling it with the energy of kindness. When you feel your deck has received all the energy it can, place it down in front of you and close your eyes for a moment as you ground your body back into the moment. Keeping your significator card where you can see it, pick up your deck and start to shuffle, pulling a card for each of the following questions:

- *Card 1:* How can I be kinder to myself?
- *Card 2:* How can I bring more kindness to my home?
- *Card 3:* How can I bring more kindness to my work?
- *Card 4:* How can I bring more kindness to my day?

I recommend doing more journal work with these cards, especially if you happened to get a card or cards that seem odd, misaligned, or confusing, such as the Tower, the Devil, the Ten of Swords, the Five of Cups, or the Moon, as they may require you to pause and dig a little deeper. Just do not reject whatever card or cards show up. Trust that it is the correct one, and it has a healing message for you regarding the devotional practice of kindness and how to bring more of it into your life. Explore why you think this card seems odd or why your first reaction is to reject it and draw another card. At this point in our work together, also notice if a triggering card keeps reappearing in the exercises. You might have a card or a few cards that have been stalking you all the way through the bottom chakras, and here in the heart, it is asking for your attention. If you feel inclined to take any triggering cards one step further, use them as a point of meditation and see what other messages these cards have for you and your healing work. Just remember, kindness does not need to be an act. It can be a way of living your entire life.

· · · · ·

## 7. Gratitude

Unless you have been living under a rock, you will have heard of gratitude work. It has become the latest and greatest tool in the hipster New Age. Now don't get me wrong, gratitude work is important and plays a role in keeping and maintaining the energy of the heart chakra, but as you have seen throughout this chapter, it is not the only area we should be focused on. One of the reasons gratitude has become so popular in the last decade is that it is linked to abundance. Many successful entrepreneurs have a gratitude story, the kind of story that gets people hooked on the idea of gratitude work as a quick fix to their financial problems. Allowing the money part to hook you means you miss the larger and deeper work gratitude does in all areas of your life. Gratitude is a way of looking at the world as if it is divinely blessed, and when we apply this lens to our own life, it helps us shift out of a lack lens into a more supported and abundant lens.

There is no doubt that the more grateful and thankful we are, the more we will see things to be grateful and thankful for. This is vital information for the heart chakra, for as the heart feels your gratitude, it sends a message to the brain telling it to be on the lookout for more things that make you feel that way. The heart keeps collecting information, the brain keeps looking out, and before you know it, your material world has morphed into a version of your perception. Gratitude is not the only energy that works this way, yet it is the one that has risen to fame in the most spectacular way. From a heart chakra perspective, gratitude is a necessary ingredient for health and well-being because of how it makes us feel and how it opens the heart center to receive more of that feeling. Gratitude is wonderful at opening our hearts, as it slowly but surely pries open our clamped and closed heart chakra and gets us to believe that we are supported and provided for.

Gratitude can be the first step to reconnecting us with our lower chakras, which we can cut off or throttle due to trauma. It is one of the reasons a lot of healers and therapists ask their clients and patients to either keep a gratitude journal or write a daily gratitude list. The very act of writing these things out connects us to the third chakra through engagement, the second chakra through memory, and the first chakra through connection. Drawing this energy down to the root and then back up to the heart is very healing as it keeps chakra energy flowing. This is really the reason I like gratitude work so much. It is because of the power it has to reconnect the bottom chakras and get energy moving again. Being healthy will top being wealthy any day, for as long as you have your health, you can achieve anything. Therefore, make sure that each and every morning, your health is on that list. Even if it is not currently where you would like it to be, put it on there anyway.

## EXERCISE

· · · · ·

Now it's time to select your gratitude significator, keeping in mind that this card must relate to a feeling of what it is to be in a state of gratitude. You might pick this card visually, allowing the images to invoke a feeling, or you may select it by your understanding of the cards themselves. Recommended cards include the Star, the Hanged Man, the Magician, any of the aces, the Three of Cups, the Nine of Pentacles, and the Six of Cups. When you have selected your card, take it to your journal and write about how this card relates to gratitude and why you feel it is the best fit for your gratitude work. This card will play a key role moving forward in how you view gratitude and how you use it to draw energy up from your lower three chakras. Keep that in mind as you do your journal work.

Once you have selected your gratitude significator, put it with your card for engagement, your card for memory, and your card for connection from the previous sections, and let's see visually how they work together. One of the fabulous things about working with tarot this way is the visual mapping magic it brings with it. Put the cards in a row as follows:

| 1 | 2 | 3 | 4 |

- *Card 1:* Heart Chakra Gratitude Significator
- *Card 2:* Solar Plexus Chakra Engagement Significator

- *Card 3:* Sacral Chakra Memory Significator
- *Card 4:* Root Chakra Connection Significator

This is how the energy is moving up and down, starting at the heart and opening up a pathway down to the root. Then, it is bringing that root energy, along with all the information from the lower chakras, back up to the heart. There really is something magical about being able to see this in the images of the cards, as it allows us to see the story that is being told inside our chakras and is a story we would not normally have access to.

What's your story? How are your chakras talking to each other while you are in the act of gratitude? This question can be answered in your journal or via meditation, though I recommend you start with your journal and see if you can come to any aha moments there first. Oftentimes, we have the most amazing breakthroughs when we give ourselves permission to just write and dump it all out on the page. Knowing how gratitude is working in your life is tremendously helpful, and now you have a visual map—a magical doorway, if you will—to how your heart communicates with your lower chakras just by finding things for which you are thankful. I think you just found something else to add to your gratitude list.

· · · · ·

## Heart Chakra Tarot Healing

Now that you have worked through the seven key issues of the fourth chakra, it is time to do some energy healing work on all that you have discovered, all that has bubbled up, and all that has presented itself for cleaning and clearing. Grab your tarot deck and get out the significator cards for the issues covered in this chapter. Select your significator card for the heart chakra and place it in front of you. This card is going to be the middle card in your heart chakra healing mandala wheel.

Your card order is as follows:

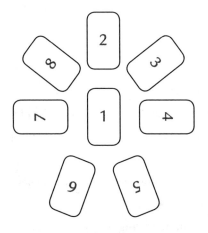

- *Card 1:* Heart Chakra Significator
- *Card 2:* Fellowship Significator
- *Card 3:* Love Significator
- *Card 4:* Empathy Significator
- *Card 5:* Compassion Significator
- *Card 6:* Forgiveness Significator
- *Card 7:* Kindness Significator
- *Card 8:* Gratitude Significator

Your center card is going to be the energy you will see flowing in and out of the other cards, as if a beautiful pink or green smoke wisps out of the card and starts to tickle the other cards around it. As we move into the visualization part of this exercise, move your hands over the cards as you say the following affirmations for each of the cards surrounding your heart chakra significator. The tarot mandala helps anchor your energy healing work and allows you to engage more fully with the overall process. Your affirmations are as follows:

- *Card 2:* I am actively supported.
- *Card 3:* I am a vessel for divine love.
- *Card 4:* I am cleaning myself so I can be of service to others.
- *Card 5:* I am constantly seeing the world through a compassionate lens.
- *Card 6:* I am holding a space of forgiveness for myself each and every day.
- *Card 7:* I am practicing the devotional art of kindness.
- *Card 8:* I am truly grateful for all that is, was, and is on its way.

Find somewhere comfortable and quiet, where you won't be disturbed for up to twenty minutes. Place your cards where you can see them and start rubbing your palms gently together as you focus on your breathing. Rub your hands together for about forty seconds, activating the energy centers in your palms. You might start to feel some heat in your hands, and this is good. Now place your hands over your heart and focus on your breath, inhaling through your nose. Feel the breath as it hits the back of your throat, fills your lungs, and expands your chest. As you exhale from the mouth, feel the breath leaving your body and deflating the lungs. Let the breath work become automatic, and shift your focus to your cards, starting with the center card, which is your heart chakra significator. Visualize the pink or green smoke gently rising from the card and twirling around the wheel you have created around it. Each time you exhale, the smoky wisps extend farther and farther. Sit like this for a few minutes, just doing the breath work and keeping your hands on your heart as you feel your chest rise and fall, and visualize the smoky pink or green energy infusing your spread.

When you feel ready, move your hands to your tarot mandala and move them along each card as you speak the corresponding affirmation statements out loud. Read through the entire list three times. Once you have finished, just relax and focus on the breath work, placing the hands back over your heart. As you inhale, feel the smoky pink or green energy coming into your nose, hitting the back of your throat, filling up your lungs, moving into your chest, and infusing the heart chakra. Relax into this, as you inhale all this lovely infused energy, letting it clean and clear your heart chakra as it embeds your affirmations into your chakra. When this feels complete, remove your hands and just breathe normally for thirty to forty seconds. Thank your cards, and you are done.

You can repeat this simple tarot healing session anytime you want, and by all means, journal about how the session made you feel or any revelations you had during the session. The more you know, the more you inquire, the more you heal.

# 5

# The Throat Chakra

The throat chakra is your fifth chakra. This chakra sits right where your neck dips, at the center of your collarbone. This energy center regulates the health of your neck, shoulders, arms, thyroid, vocal cords, esophagus, trachea, mouth, and parathyroid gland. It is often referred to as your communication center, as it deals with how we speak, listen, hear, and navigate the task of receiving and giving information. Inside this chapter you are going to explore seven issues the throat chakra deals with on a consistent and ongoing bases. These seven issues each have their own section in this chapter, as they all have important information for you regarding the health and well-being of your throat chakra.

The sections are as follows:

1. Listening

2. Speaking

3. Hearing and Being Heard

4. Giving and Receiving

5. Decision-Making

6. Consent

7. Reading and Writing

## Vishuddha

The throat chakra, also known as *vishuddha,* deals with both inner and outer dialogue, and as you move through this chapter, you will see just how good your communication skills are. Most people struggle with clear, concise communication. In my energy healing practice, I have seen partners, lovers, and family members who are unable to talk about things that really matter but get very hooked to things that don't matter at all. Technology (and its offshoot, social media) is both a blessing and a curse to the energy of the throat chakra. For some, it has opened up a whole new world in which to communicate, whereas for others, it has made them afraid to open their mouths for fear of being publicly judged and shamed by people they don't even know. We have access to more varied forms of communication than ever before, which means we have more ways to be bombarded with noise, messages, and mass media.

Keep in mind that how we communicate is not just an outside job, and by that I mean most people focus primarily on audible speech, such as words coming out of the mouth and being heard by another. The throat chakra is heavily influenced by our inner speech as well. That is the dialogue that is constantly running inside our mind. We all talk to ourselves. You're probably doing it right now as you read this book. It is the daily exchange we have with ourselves that does the most damage to our throat chakra, as we tend to save the vilest rants for the spaces where other people can't hear them. Language is a fascinating thing, and how, when, and why you use it will impact your throat chakra, either in a positive healing way or a destructive and damaging way. This is why it does not surprise me that the suit of swords in the tarot is often connected to communication. Swords, like words, are sharp, dangerous things. They can wound or liberate, depending on how they are used. They can empower and inspire or diminish and reduce a person's life force energy. Words, like the suit of swords, can bring pain and suffering or give us ways to rejoice and rediscover who we are and why we are here. As you have learned so far in this book, there are lots of ways to communicate. You can do it verbally, emotionally, physically, mentally, or vibrationally, and all these ways are regulated right here in the throat chakra.

## EXERCISE
· · · · ·

It's time to find your throat chakra significator. This card should align with how you communicate. Are you a verbal communicator, an emotional, tactical communicator, or a physical, waving-your-arms-and-hands-around communicator? Are you a vibrationally impacted communicator, picking up on all the subtle energies around you and using them as a way to have a dialogue with the world around you? Really think about this before you select a card, as it will make a big difference in the types of cards you will be attracted to. You may also need to consider how good you feel you are at communication. Are you always clearly understood, or are people constantly misunderstanding what you are trying to convey to them? I highly recommend using the court cards for this significator exercise, as they show you steps and stages. You might be a Knight of Cups, learning to emotionally communicate with the world at large, or perhaps you are the Queen of Swords, always getting straight to the point, so there is no room for confusion. Are you perhaps the King of Wands, the life of the party and a smooth talker who is always getting their way, since you know how to connect on a vibrational level? This significator card really should be an honest representation of how you feel about your ability to hear, listen, speak, and decide. If you have room to be better and learn more, then perhaps you need to look at the pages and the knights. However, if you know you are a silver-tongued magician, then I recommend you look at the queens and the kings.

Once you have selected your card, take it to your journal and write about why it is a true and accurate portrait of the current energy surrounding your throat chakra. Write freely for as long as you can, exploring the ways in which the figure in the card you have selected would speak, listen, and make decisions. Think about creating a list of these words and start including them in your own speech, both in conversations with others and when talking to yourself. Take your time with these exercises, and you might even find you stretch it out over a couple of days. This is perfectly fine, just as long as it is done from a place of healing and exploration and not a place of self-flagellation. Keep that heart chakra open and be kind and compassionate with yourself as you dive deeper into your throat chakra.

. . . . .

## 1. Listening

You do not need to be able to hear in order to listen. Take for example those in our community who are deaf or suffer from a severe hearing impairment. They are more than capable of listening, even if they cannot hear. Listening is a form of engagement; it is being present with information and truly allowing yourself to become a part of it. Listening is done with both our physical ears and our inner or middle ears. When spirit, gods, guides, and intuition talk to us, it is usually through whispers in our middle ear, as this is where vibration is amplified. In this section we are not going to get into how the ear works, as we will save that for our section on hearing. In this section, our primary focus is on how the act of listening is an important function of the throat chakra.

Listening is becoming a bit of a dying art form. With more and more noise vying for our attention, people's attention spans aren't as long as they used to be. This means that if you have to spend your time actively engaged in something, someone else is saying that it must be worth your time, energy, and effort. I am an active listener, and one of my pet peeves is when someone turns on the television or puts some music on and then wants to have a conversation over the competing noise. When I'm having a conversation with someone, I would like our words to be our primary focus so we can honor each other through the acts of listening, sharing, and participating in each other's stories.

Unfortunately, this is not how a lot of people communicate. If I'm listening to music, I would like to get lost in that music and allow it to move me in some way. If I am watching television, I would like my focus to be on what I am watching and not on who else is in the room. I can even describe what the sound of our neighborhood is, as I listen to it every morning as I write, just me, my laptop, my cat, and the open window. Birds sing, the breeze blows, and traffic steadily increases as the day transitions from dawn to the morning rush hour. All these sounds are competing for my attention, which means all are contributing the information they are sharing. We bombard ourselves on a daily basis with noise for noise's sake, which has made it difficult for the throat chakra to participate in the vital act of listening. One can't multitask while listening. You are either present, focused, and engaged, or you are not. Your throat chakra knows when you are actively listening and when you are not, and it is sensitive to the subtle differences in our ears.

How well do you believe you listen?

## EXERCISE
· · · · ·

Pick up your deck, hold it between your hands, and imagine a turquoise light coming out of your throat and slowly wrapping around the deck of cards in your hand. Take a few deep, grounding breaths and just imagine this light blue or turquoise light infusing the cards with the energy of your throat chakra. Take another nice, deep breath and slowly begin to shuffle your cards. As you shuffle, just repeat the following statement three times: "I'm listening to this message from my throat chakra." Now fan the cards out in front of you, face down, and select one card and one card only. This card is your current listening significator. Do not redraw it if you don't like the card or find the card confusing. Just trust that this is exactly the card you need to work with right now to assist you and your throat chakra.

If you selected a major arcana card, your throat has a specific issue or skill it would like you to focus on. If you selected a court card, the throat chakra is letting you know how you are currently approaching the act of listening, and it is either as a child, a young adult, a mature adult, or a fully engaged, present, wise adult. If you selected your card from one of the suits of the minor arcana, you are being shown how you are currently prioritizing your listening abilities. You either pay attention more to emotional language and information in the cups, written or educational information in the swords, active and physical information in the pentacles, and spiritual or desire-based information in the wands.

Take this card to your journal and do as much free writing about your card and how it relates to listening as you feel you need. Consider exploring how this card can be used to refine your listening abilities or improve your current skill set. Once you have written as much as you can off the top of your head, pick up one or two of your favorite tarot books and see what they have to say about your card. Keep in mind that you are looking for information that is relevant to the act of listening, attention, focus, and engagement, so look for key words or phrases that may be helpful for your point of inquiry. Once you have even more information for your card, can you see clearly the message your throat chakra has for you? If, for whatever reason, it is still unclear to you or you would like addition information, by all means go ahead and pull a couple more cards. Two to three should suffice. Use the same journal technique for the additional cards, and keep the information relevant to the issue of this section, since all you really need to discover is just how good of a listener you truly are.

· · · · ·

## 2. Speaking

Are you a talker or a someone who prefers silence? The throat chakra, I have found, tends to be an extreme chakra, meaning it is either fully open and hyperactive, or it is quiet and barely moves. People tend to be the same. They are either talkers or nontalkers. People either have to constantly keep adding noise to a space via their mouths, or they sit in silence. Talkers and nontalkers are very different people. They process the world differently, and they engage with it differently. Nontalkers tend to be more observant and aware, as they spend more time examining their surroundings and assessing information visually and audibly than their constantly talking counterparts. Talkers tend to miss a lot of information, usually because they are never quiet long enough to hear it or receive it. Yet, at the same time, they do have skills in asking constant questions, which does tend to reap them more information than they know what to do with. I'm a nontalker, and my wife is a talker. I do not find a need to vocalize each and every aspect of my life, and in fact, most days I walk through the world silently. My wife talks from the moment her eyes open until they close. She talks to everything, including the bed, the windows, the cat, her food, the plants, and sometimes even to me. The world is a very different place for talkers and nontalkers. This is why knowing which one you are is important.

Talking in and of itself is not necessarily a bad thing. Vocalizing, speaking up, and being heard are all power elements of the throat chakra. Talking is only a problem when it is used for gossip, for malice, and as a weapon. There is no doubt that our voice can be a very powerful tool. In kundalini yoga, teachers advise students to use their voice as a healing vessel. In her audiobook *Invincible Living*, Guru Jagat speaks of how her teacher Yogi Bhajan believed that our own personal sound current is the most healing and transformative sound current we can experience while in physical form.[11] Some people can sing so beautifully they move people to tears. Other people can speak so passionately that they create movements and make massive change in the world.

Gossip, however, is an insidious product of the throat chakra. It is like a cancer that spreads, grows, and infects as it invades the world. Gossiping pulls all your fears and doubts up from the chakras below and spews them out into the world as a nasty narrative about someone else. This sort of speaking and communicating can damage the throat chakra and over time can cause problems in the mouth as well. Lying is another form of suppression or damaging of the throat chakra, because it is not using the chakra energy as it was designed to be used, which is to speak one's truth.

Technology has changed the way we speak and are spoken to. In my experience it appears that more words are exchanged through social media, email, and our phones than they are via our mouths. The language we use has been changed with the advent of smart phones, along with the way we communicate. It has become short, concise, quick, and as impersonal as possible. How many messages do you get that are just emojis? I know even I have fallen to the emoji response. This new way of communicating and the way we tend to relate to each other via social media, email, and text message has also changed the energy around the throat chakra, yet the energy itself has stayed the same, and that means it still needs to be balanced, empowered, and healed, the way it has always been.

---

11. Guru Jagat, *Invincible Living: The Power of Yoga, the Energy of Breath, and Other Tools for a Radiant Life* (San Francisco, CA: HarperOne, 2017).

## EXERCISE

· · · · ·

In order to work further on your throat, you will first need a significator card for this section, and it will be one that reflects if you are a talker or a nontalker. It will be a card that shows if you like to have a captive audience when you speak or if you prefer an intimate, one-on-one conversation. Your card should be a reflection of your current talking state, so you will select this significator while looking at the cards, searching the images and artwork for a picture that best represents how you see yourself, either as a talker or nontalker. Recommended cards include the High Priestess, the Ten of Pentacles, the Ten of Cups, the Four of Pentacles, the Nine of Pentacles, the Five of Swords, the Three of Swords, and the Nine of Cups.

Once you have selected your card, take it to your journal and contemplate how this card works in an active and passive way. Also, consider the positive and negative aspects of this card in terms of how you speak, when you speak, and why you speak. Write as much as you can freely and off the top of your head, before picking up your favorite tarot books and exploring the meaning of the card further. If you would like to go even deeper with this card, try the following quick automatic writing exercise. Place the card somewhere you can see it and, resting your gaze on it, take in the whole image with your eyes. Then, ask the card, "How do you use me as a vessel and speak through me?" Pick up your pen and write down the reply. Just write whatever pops into your head. Don't worry if it makes sense or not—

just write it. This will help give you even more insight into how your throat chakra energy is working in you and through you. Try not to judge anything that comes up, but see it for what it is, which is information that can, and will, be used to assist you in your betterment.

· · · · ·

## 3. Hearing and Being Heard

Sound moves in and around the ear, allowing us to hear. The working of the ear is quite fascinating. Vibrations dance down the ear canal into the eardrum and then hit the middle ear or ear bones. Our ears are quite the little echo chambers, taking unseen waves of vibrational energy and turning them into what we call sound. Our ears are also very adaptable, as I learned at great length when my youngest child was going through ear infection after ear infection, which ultimately resulted in surgery. My youngest heard most of her sounds through a muffled, swollen eardrum, relying on her middle ear to do all the hard work of putting sound together in a clear and concise way. She was incredibly blessed to not have lost her hearing, and her speech was in no way affected. She was lucky, but many are not.

This connection between hearing and speech is something most of us take for granted. In fact, we rarely even think about it. However, how we hear, especially as infants and toddlers, has an incredible effect on how we speak and, in turn, how we are heard. Our need to be heard can come from multiple factors. It may come from having hearing issues as a small child, or it may come from being the lone, lost voice in a loud and noisy house filled with siblings. Either way, your hearing, or what you could and could not hear, has affected how you now speak and how you feel you are being heard in the world around you, and all of this is connected to your throat chakra.

## EXERCISE
· · · · ·

In the previous section of this chapter, you selected a speaking significator, and here in this section, we need to find its working partner by selecting a hearing significator. Grab your deck, and let's see if you can find a card that best represents your hearing abilities. As you select this card, I want you to focus on how you like to be heard. Do you like to be the big booming voice over a noisy crowd like the King of Wands or Emperor? Or do you like to have the noise of the room drop to your level so you can remain quiet and still, like the Star or the Moon? Perhaps you're more of a casual conversationalist, so you don't mind there being a few mingling voices, as long as they are not competing for noise, like in the Three of Cups, the Four of Wands, and the Ten of Pentacles. Maybe you prefer not to be heard at all, shrinking into the background, hoping no one will pay you any attention, like the Hermit, the Eight of Cups, the Two of Wands, or even the Hanged Man. I highly suggest you work with the artwork on the card when selecting your significator card, as trying to find it with the card meanings alone might be difficult, if you are not overly proficient with the tarot card meanings.

These two significator cards, speaking and being heard, work hand in hand every second of every day, even if you are hearing impaired or legally deaf. Lay your two significators down in front of you, face up.

These two cards are a pair and should be read as such. Working in pairs is not traditionally a tarot practice and is normally delegated to the Lenormand, but I am a big fan of the tarot magical pair reading, which is exactly what we are going to do here. Pairings work differently, depending on how you position the cards; the meanings will change when you switch the cards around. In other words, the first pairing shows how your hearing impacts how you speak, and the second pairing shows how your speaking affects how you are heard.

Spend time exploring both of these pairings, as they will give you different readings. Consider writing in your journal about a time in your past when you saw these cards, in both positions, being played out. It might have been at a party, a conference, a work meeting or even just at home with your family. In this respect, you would use the first card as a noun or identifier and the second card as an adjective or descriptor. Have fun with this, and don't linger on it for too long. You want to do this short pairing exercise quickly, using the first words that come to mind. If you need to, set a timer and give yourself only three to five minutes on each task.

Take these cards one step further, and turn it into a tarot spread by adding the significator for the throat chakra and lay it out like so:

- *Card 1:* Hearing Significator
- *Card 2:* Speaking Significator
- *Card 3:* Throat Chakra Significator

Now you can visually see how this simple act of communication, hearing, and speaking, is working with your throat chakra energy. You can see how the magical pairing is influencing the larger environment in which they express themselves. I highly recommend that after doing these exercises, you spend some time in your journal reviewing this information and seeing how you can either make improvements or create new, and healthier, communication habits. Perhaps you are not being heard the way you would like to be, and the cards have some very useful information on how to assist you in healing that. Maybe you have noticed that you are not really paying attention, and your hearing is causing you to speak at inappropriate times. Just make sure you use this information for healing the throat and not for beating yourself up. End your journal work in this section by saying, "Thank you, throat chakra, for all you have communicated to me as I make my way through my findings." This small act will change the way you look at, and feel about, the information you have gathered. Communication is just sharing information, but information is power, and here the power is healing. Thank you, throat chakra, for allowing this healing to take place.

• • • • •

## 4. Giving and Receiving

I am guessing that if you are familiar with the chakras already, you did not expect to see the issue of giving and receiving here in the throat chakra, yet this is exactly what this chakra teaches us. When we listen, we receive; when we talk, we give. Just as when we are heard, we are received, and when we hear others, we give. Effective, clear, concise communication is all about giving and receiving. It is a form of energy exchange from one person to another, or sometimes from ourselves to ourselves. The healthier the throat chakra, the more giving and receptive someone is. Now, please don't confuse a healthy throat chakra with someone who talks all the time, as we discussed in the second section of this chapter. Overuse of the throat chakra is just as damaging as underutilization, or not speaking when one needs to, to this chakra's energy. A healthy throat chakra is one that understands that sometimes there is a time to speak, and sometimes there is a time to listen. People with well-functioning throat chakras do not need to dominate conversations, nor are they terrified to open their mouths and breathe. They have worked out a balance, a give and take, and a way to exchange energy between themselves and the world of noise around them. They honor both the speaker and the listener. They understand the importance of giving and receiving.

Marisa Peer, founder of Rapid Transformational Therapy, does an exercise in which she asks people to take a breath and to just keep taking it, never letting it go. When you can't possibly take a breath in anymore, she stops you and then asks you to let your breath go, and to just keep letting it go until you almost pass out.[12] The point of this exercise is to show people that we are naturally programmed to give and receive. We take in oxygen when we breathe, and we give back carbon dioxide. If you are a nature-based healer, witch, or priestess, you would already honor this exchange by giving thanks to the trees, since the trees give us what we need, and we give the trees what they need. They give us oxygen, and we give them carbon dioxide. Giving and receiving is as important as the very breath we take to stay alive. This breath, funnily enough, needs the throat to be able to get it in and out of the lungs. What I love about Peer's exercise is that it allows us to look at all areas of our life and ask, "Where am I taking a breath and giving it back?" and "Where in my life am I giving my breath but forgetting to take one in return?" Being able to align giving and receiving energy with breath work is ingenious, as we can all relate to the desperate and primal need to breathe.

## EXERCISE
· · · · ·

As we move on to find a significator for this energy, you will need to keep something in mind. Your card has to show giving in one aspect and receiving in the other. That means it might show giving when upright but receiving when reversed, or it may show receiving when upright and giving when reversed. This is going to stretch what you know about the tarot cards, which is why I want you to focus on the art of the image before you move into the meaning of the card itself. Look for

---

12. Marisa Peer, "Do This to Completely HEAL Your Mind and Body," Mind-Valley Talks, September 6, 2019, YouTube video, 51:39, https://www.you tube.com/watch?v=egbiGhAiN8E&feature=youtu.be, min. 38–39.

images or artwork that show this giving energy. The Six of Pentacles is an example of this. In one position, we can clearly see an offering, and in the other, we can envision a receiving. This could also be true of the aces, the Empress, the Ten of Pentacles, the Nine of Cups, the Seven of Swords, Temperance, and Judgement. If you are really new to tarot and this is proving challenging, I recommend sticking with the aces, as their simple artwork, especially in decks based very strictly around the Rider-Waite-Smith original, is much easier to work with for this task.

Before you begin the journal process of this exercise, think about how this card relates to the simple exchange of inhaling and exhaling, as well as the need to keep the body alive and strong through the subconscious act of giving and receiving. You may even stop to imagine how this card feels to you as you breathe, holding it upright when you inhale and flipping it upside down when you exhale. Watch as the image turns and shifts as you take each breath. Upright, inhale. Reversed, exhale. The slower the breath, the more time you spend with each aspect of the card.

Now, take it to your journal and start writing about why you chose this card above all others. What is it about the acts of giving and receiving that speak to you in the artwork of this card, especially if you have selected a specific suit? Cups may indicate you are an emotional giver and receiver, swords may indicate you are an intellectual giver and receiver, wands may represent you as an action-oriented giver and receiver, and the pentacles reflect a more down-to-earth and practical giver and receiver. Write freely for as long as you can. Then move on to your tarot book and see what further information you can gain about your cards. Remember to only gather information that is relevant to the acts of giving and receiving.

You may even wish to pair this card with your throat chakra significator and do the magical pairs exercise from the previous section with these two cards. Do the magical pairs once with both cards upright and once with both cards in the reversed aspect. This will give even more information on how this giving and receiving energy is working with your throat chakra to help maintain a happy, balanced, and healthy energy. The more information we have, the deeper the healing work we can do.

· · · · ·

## 5. Decision-Making

Are you a yes-person or a no-person? Whichever one you are, it has created a vortex of energy in your throat chakra. This vortex has made your decision-making a bit of a habit, as your throat will make an automatic response. Now you might think your decision-making happens in your head, and while the problem-solving aspect of it does, the answer we vocalize, most times out of habit, is all from the throat. Have you ever had one of those moments when before you knew what happened, you agreed to something that, given the time and thought, you would never have agreed to? Have you ever said no to something before you gave yourself a chance to contemplate the long-term consequences of your answer? We all have done both of these things, as our throat has an energetic trigger response programmed into it, one we put in there through years and years of saying yes and no.

You hear people discuss what their head says and what their heart says, but no one ever discusses what their throat says. This is mainly because the complexities of the throat chakra are often overlooked. Most think our throat is one of the simpler chakras, one that doesn't deal with too many heavy issues, and one that is just about communication. Raise your voice, share your song, and all will be right with this energy center. This is just not true, and the decision-making component of the throat chakra is so very important to acknowledge and understand, as it truly does affect every aspect of our day-to-day lives.

This is why knowing if you are predominately a yes-person or a no-person is important, because your responses to all options presented to you throughout your life have created a preset script in your throat chakra. This information gathered from your throat is stored in the brain, so when it comes to a problem that needs to be solved or an opportunity that may be presented to you, it runs through the information the throat has collected and works in tandem with the trigger response your throat has created. We are nothing more than parrots in that respect, constantly running on preprogramed responses—responses that we created. I can't emphasize this enough, because this has nothing to do with anyone outside of yourself. The finger can only be pointed at yourself. The liberating part of this, however, is that because you did this, you can also undo it. You can become more aware of the energy, the habits, and the triggers in your throat chakra and choose to reprogram it in a way that is more empowering and life-affirming.

# EXERCISE

· · · · ·

For this section, the Sun card is going to be your significator. It is also now going to be your yes or no card in your tarot deck. Upright will be yes and reversed will be no. The sun in your sky is both a giver and a destroyer of life. We could not live without the sun, and it is the reason our food grows. At the same time, not only can too much time in the sun kill us, but it can also kill the plants, trees, and grasses that produce our food. The Sun card holds this energy in it. It represents the joy of life and the need to honor your life-giving energy by setting up some very clear boundaries. In other words, the Sun card lets us know when to say yes to life-giving energy and when to say no or "that's enough" when that energy threatens to take the very gift it once supplied.

Remove your Sun card from your deck and place it in the upright position on your meditation altar or somewhere you can see it while you sit. Get yourself comfortable and gaze at your Sun card while you take some nice, deep, grounding breaths. Feel your body settle into the moment as you keep gazing at your Sun card. As you continue the breath work, bring to mind the last time you were faced with a decision you really wanted to say yes to but instead said no to. This is a situation or experience that lit you up and got you excited, but you declined it anyway. Keep this situation and experience in your mind, hold it as you keep gazing at the Sun card, and move your right hand to cover your throat chakra. You don't have to physically touch your body; just hover over the chakra area. Now repeat the word *yes* seven times, keeping your hand over the throat chakra. Just take in a couple of nice, deep breaths and let the image go. Remove your hand and turn your Sun card upside down.

Settle back in your seated position, and once again gaze at your card while just working the breath by breathing in through the nose and out through the mouth. Once you feel connected back to your card, place your right hand over your throat chakra. Bring to mind a situation in which you said yes but in all honesty should have said no, as saying yes only bought more problems and maybe caused you to feel totally out of alignment with yourself. Once you have that situation or experience firmly in your mind's eye, say the world *no* seven times. Keeping your hand over the throat chakra, just take in a couple of nice, deep breaths and let the image go. Now imagine a beautiful turquoise light flowing out of the palm of your right hand and creating a wonderful budding flower on your throat. See if you can imagine it opening and blooming. If possible, take in as much detail as you can, and notice if you can smell its scent in the air around you. Sit with this energy flowing in and through your throat chakra for a couple of minutes. Then, keeping your hand over your throat chakra, just take in a couple of nice, deep breaths and let the image go. Now drop your hand and relax back into the present moment.

This short and simple exercise will help in reprogramming your decision-making center. It will also make it easier for you to identify situations that are clearly yes ones and those that are a definite no. Repeat this meditation with your Sun card as often as you like. Just make sure you do the complete meditation with the card both right-side up and reversed, as this is important. May the Sun now guide you on your way.

• • • • •

## 6. Consent

As a society, we don't think about consent enough. Consent is about giving permission for something to happen. It is to accept, allow, agree, approve, submit, and give in to. We consent to things all the time without being fully aware of them. A nod of the head here, a shrug of the shoulders there and a "Sure, why not?" in between. Yet, consent is more than saying yes: it is an agreement and one that will have future consequences. We consent to how we allow others to treat us, and we consent to the way we treat ourselves. We consent to the life we have created, whether we enjoy it or not. We have, at some point, consented to the conditions of our daily existence, regardless of if they are life-affirming or life-draining.

More than likely, most often when you give consent, you are doing so out of habit. As we discussed in the previous section of this chapter, the throat chakra learns your yesses and your nos and starts to automate your verbal responses based on years of information gathering. It also starts to do this with consent. If you have spent years beating yourself up and dragging yourself down, you have given consent to be treated badly by yourself, and you have entered into an agreement with yourself in which you are willing to accept this as normal and you will submit to your abusive behavior. The same is true with allowing toxic people into our lives: if you do it often enough, it becomes habitual. The good news is that anything that has been programed can be reprogramed, and habits aren't set in stone. This means they can, and are meant to be, changed and refined over time. So anything you have given consent to, in this life or any other that came before it, can be undone, and a new agreement can be put into place.

## EXERCISE
• • • • •

To begin this process, you will need to deliberately select a consent significator, a card that represents you being in control and confident with your voice. Each and every time you look at this card, you will instantly feel like you are consenting to your highest and best good. Recommended cards for this are the Sun, Justice, the World, the King and Queen of Swords, the King and Queen of Wands, Strength, and the High Priestess. Now that you have your significator card, put it in front of you face up so you can see it. Grab your deck of cards and hold it between your hands. Take a moment to settle your breath and imagine a turquoise or light blue light coming out of your throat chakra. See it swirling around your deck of cards. Take another nice, deep breath, and see this turquoise or blue light infusing your cards, filling them up with throat chakra energy. When you feel ready, begin to shuffle slowly, asking each question out loud as you pull one card per each of the following questions:

- *CS:* Consent Significator
- *Card 1:* What sort of consent have I given to my body?

- *Card 2:* What sort of consent have I given to my finances?
- *Card 3:* What sort of consent have I given to my partner or family?
- *Card 4:* What sort of consent have I given to myself?

Lay your cards out as follows:

```
        ┌─────┐
        │  1  │
        └─────┘

┌─────┐ ┌─────┐ ┌─────┐
│  4  │ │  S  │ │  2  │
└─────┘ └─────┘ └─────┘

        ┌─────┐
        │  3  │
        └─────┘
```

If you do not already have writing material, grab a pen and paper or your journal so you can take some notes. As you glance over the spread in front of you, what's the first thing to stand out, that one thing that catches your eye above everything else? Start your notes by explaining why you think this is the first thing to seek your attention. From there, go on and explore the rest of the cards in the spread, starting with doing free writing off the top of your head for as long as you can. Make sure you use the words that go with consent in your findings, such as *accept, give permission, allow, approve*, and *submit*. Even consider using these words to start your sentences. For example, "In card 1, I see that I have given permission to my body" or "Card 3 shows me that I have approved of this behavior from a partner or family member." The more you use and get comfortable with the language of consent, the more you will become aware of it when it pops up. Use the language as much as possible, as you continue your journal work with this spread. Even when you turn to your favorite tarot books, be on the lookout for consent language, in regard to the cards that you have selected for the spread.

If you want a more complete collection of consent language, go online and search for "define consent." This will bring up all you will need for the above exercise. The more awareness you have, the better your ability to reprogram your throat chakra. The more you understand how consent is working in your life, the more you can cut, clear, and delete all agreements and contracts you have consented to that no longer serve you. Understanding this component of the throat chakra is liberating, as it can, and does, free you from energy that is holding you back, blocking your path or smothering your light. You may have needed to consent to something at some point in your life, but you don't have to consent to it now, and the here and now is the only place that currently matters.

· · · · ·

## 7. Reading and Writing

Up until now, we have primarily focused on the audible aspect of the throat chakra, as in the noises made through the throat or inner dialogue we hear inside our heads. In this section, however, we turn our attention to the last two forms of communication that the throat chakra deals with, which are reading and writing. There is no doubt that the more a person reads, the better they write and the more words they have at their disposal when it is time to open their mouth. However, not everyone has access to books, and not everyone enjoys writing. Some of us even have a rocky start in the reading and writing department. I was one of those people. I had terrible problems with reading as a child, even though I loved books, which in turn meant my writing was horrible. I was told I would also have subpar language skills and that I needed to look into professions that didn't involve a lot of written work. I think you can see how that worked out for me. However, I swallowed that crap for the first thirty-eight years of my life, which is why we have to be very careful of what we continuously tell children about our perceptions of what their limitations may be.

I don't tell you my story just because I love writing about myself. I tell you my story because what happens to us in childhood can block this area of our throat chakra. If you didn't have access to books, so you told yourself they were not important, that could have caused a block here. If you struggled with spelling or grammar or even suffered from dyslexia, then the story other adults may have told you could have damaged this part of your throat chakra. If you have tried and failed at journal writing (which I also did, by the way), you may think that writing is not for you. Perhaps you were told that poetry, fiction, and writing were a waste of your energy and that it was time to pull your head out of the clouds and get to the serious nature of adult life. There are so many ways that this part of your throat chakra can be blocked, torn, and repressed, most of them in a cruel manner. All of them stopped you from exploring how you wish to speak and be heard in the world, and they may have made you fearful to use your authentic voice.

When we are told often enough that our authentic voice is broken, not good enough, disabled, problematic, or better left unheard, this causes problems in all areas of our life and throughout the rest of our chakra system. This is why the journaling part of this book is so crucial. We have been working with healing the throat chakra all the way through this book. Each exercise is geared to get you to tap into that authentic voice and to slowly but surely create a unique and new vibration in the writing and reading part of your throat chakra energy. This entire book is a reading and writing exercise.

## EXERCISE
· · · · ·

As you think about your relationship with reading and writing, it is time to select your significator for this section. Grab your deck and start looking for images that align with how you see yourself sharing your voice through writing and reading. If the deck you are using doesn't have cards that feel like they fulfill that description, perhaps think about finding images outside your tarot deck that portray knowledge or confidence or even deep thought. Then see if you can align them to cards inside your tarot deck. The important thing is that the image makes sense to you. It must align with how you see this part of yourself in power and expressing yourself without limit and fear. Some suggested cards are the Hierophant, the High Priestess, the Queen of Swords, the Knight of Swords, the Ace of Swords, the Page of

Wands, the Four of Pentacles, or the Three of Wands. Once you have selected your card, take it to your journal and write about why this card calls to you. It doesn't even have to make logical sense. Just write whatever pops into your head. Write for as long as you can, and when you run out of things to say, gather up your favorite tarot books and hunt for even more information. Keep the information relevant to the issue of writing and reading.

If you wish to go deeper with this exercise, pair this card with your hearing and being heard significator from a previous section in this chapter and do a magical pairs reading. See how these two cards work together. Keep in mind, pairings work differently, depending on how you position the cards. The meanings will change when you switch the cards around, so consider how you wish to read these two cards together. Do you wish to have the hearing and speaking card first or second? The instructions on how to do the magical pairs reading are in the hearing and speaking section of this chapter.

Now if you are brave enough and want an even bigger picture on how speaking, hearing, and reading and writing work together as one energy here in the throat chakra, grab your speaking significator, and add it to your magical pair. Now you have a very illuminating three-card spread:

```
┌─────┐  ┌─────┐  ┌─────┐
│     │  │     │  │     │
│  1  │  │  2  │  │  3  │
│     │  │     │  │     │
└─────┘  └─────┘  └─────┘
```

- *Card 1:* Hearing Significator
- *Card 2:* Writing and Reading Significator
- *Card 3:* Speaking Significator

These three cards give you a wonderful visual of how energy is moving and working together inside your throat chakra, and how all parts of this chakra are coming together to activate, heal, and energize your throat. These cards are the blossoming flower of your throat chakra, bursting forth and unfurling. Depending on your cards, you will be able to see if you are doing this in a gentle way or a strong and forceful way, or if you are merely allowing this chakra flower to move as it sees fit. The suit, numbers, and ranking of the cards you have in this spread will also let you know if you are comfortable with opening up this energy center or if you are still struggling to allow it to be noticed. Either way, celebrate the information you have gathered here. Bless it, thank it, and let it know that you will honor it by continuing to clean and clear your center of communication.

· · · · ·

## Throat Chakra Tarot Healing

Now that you have worked through the seven key issues of the fifth chakra, it is time to do some energy healing work on all that you have discovered, all that has bubbled up, and all that has presented itself for cleaning and clearing. Grab your tarot deck and get out the significator cards for the issues covered in this chapter. Select your significator card for the throat chakra and place it in front of you. This card is going to be the middle card in your throat chakra healing mandala wheel.

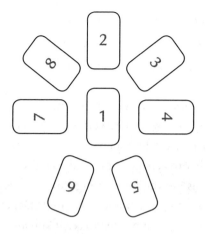

Your card order is as follows:

- *Card 1:* Throat Chakra Significator
- *Card 2:* Listening Significator
- *Card 3:* Speaking Significator
- *Card 4:* Hearing and Being Heard Significator
- *Card 5:* Giving and Receiving Significator
- *Card 6:* Decision-Making Significator
- *Card 7:* Consent Significator
- *Card 8:* Writing and Reading Significator

Your center card is going to be the energy you will see flowing in and out of the other cards, as if a beautiful turquoise smoke wisps out of the card and starts to tickle the other cards around it. As we move into the visualization part of this exercise, move your hands over the cards as you say the following affirmations for each of the cards surrounding your throat chakra significator. The tarot mandala helps anchor your energy healing work and allows you to engage more fully with the overall process. Your affirmations are as follows:

- *Card 2:* I am listening.
- *Card 3:* I am using my voice when and where I need to.
- *Card 4:* I am allowing myself to be heard as I also hear others.
- *Card 5:* I am allowing information to flow in as easily as it flows out.
- *Card 6:* I am good at making decisions.
- *Card 7:* I am aware of the agreements I make and the consent I give.
- *Card 8:* I am giving myself permission to read more and write freely.

Find somewhere comfortable and quiet, where you won't be disturbed for up to twenty minutes. Place your cards where you can see them and start rubbing your palms gently together as you focus on your breathing. Rub your hands together for about forty seconds, activating the energy centers in your palms. You might start to feel some heat in your hands, and this is good. Now place your hands over your throat and focus on your breath, inhaling through your nose. Feel the breath, as it hits the back of your throat, fills your lungs, and expands your chest. As you exhale from the mouth, feel the breath leaving your body and deflating the lungs. Let the breath work become automatic, and shift your focus to your cards, starting with the center card, which is your throat chakra significator. Visualize the turquoise smoke gently rising from the card and twirling around the wheel you have created around it. Each time you exhale, the smoky wisps extend farther and farther. Sit like this for a few minutes, just doing the breath work and keeping your hands on your throat area as you feel your chest rise and fall, and visualize the smoky turquoise energy infusing your spread.

When you feel ready, move your hands to your tarot mandala and move them along each card as you speak the corresponding affirmation statements out loud. Read through the entire list three times. Once you have finished, just relax and focus on the breath work, placing your hands back over your throat. As you inhale, feel the smoky turquoise energy coming into your nose, hitting the back of your throat, and infusing the throat chakra. Relax into this, as you inhale all this lovely infused energy, letting it clean and clear your throat chakra as it embeds your affirmations into your chakra. When this feels complete, remove your hands and just breathe normally for thirty to forty seconds. Thank your cards, and you are done.

You can repeat this simple tarot healing session anytime you want, and by all means, journal about how the session made you feel or any revelations you had during the session. The more you know, the more you inquire, the more you heal.

# 6

# The Third Eye Chakra

The third eye chakra is the chakra located in the middle of your forehead. It is connected to your physical eyes, the pituitary gland, the brow, and the base of the skull and can affect your sinuses. This chakra is the pop star of the twenty-first century, as everyone wants to open their third eye. So much emphasis has been placed on this chakra over the course of the last few decades that it has stopped people from actively engaging in the lower chakras. The irony, however, is that the better condition your lower chakras are in, the more sight your third eye has. It is an inconvenient truth that if we truly wish to open our third eye and keep it open, we must work our way up through all the chakras that came before it. In this chapter, you are going to explore seven issues the third eye chakra deals with on a consistent and ongoing basis. These seven issues each have their own section in this chapter, as they all have important information for you regarding the health and well-being of your third eye chakra.

The sections are as follows:

1. Intuition

2. Future

3. Dreams

4. Sight

5. Perception

6. Bias

7. Clarity

## Ajna

The third eye chakra, or *ajna,* as it is known in Sanskrit, is a complex chakra, yet it doesn't interfere with as much of our overall health and well-being in a physical sense as its lower counterparts can. The tool, known as second sight, is best used when it can guide us toward a state of healing awareness, so that we can see things that may be eluding us along our healing path. Sure, being able to see angels and spirit guides and get glimpses of possible future events is fun, but unless there is a more meaningful purpose to the seeing, you aren't really tapping the third eye as a form of service to yourself and those around you.

The third eye also has deep connections to ancestral lineages, and people who struggle with this chakra center may come from a family line where the women were persecuted for their gift of sight. The seer has been praised and persecuted throughout history, and I don't doubt history will repeat itself. For now, we live in a time when it is safe to work with our third eye chakra, which is why it is more important than ever that we learn and teach how to do it correctly as part of a larger energy network and not a single entity. As you will see throughout this chapter, there are many areas of the third eye that need to be explored, examined, and healed. However, first we need to find a significator card for this chakra.

## EXERCISE
· · · · ·

Grab your deck and start looking for a card that you feel best represents the energy of the third eye chakra, or the energy of the third eye chakra you wish to have once your healing work is further along. Recommended cards for this chakra include the High Priestess, the Hanged Man, the Moon, or any of the queens. Do your best to select this card visually before diving into the meaning of the card itself. Once you have your significator card, reverse it and make it stand on its head. This is the true direction of sight, upside down.

Once you have selected your card, take it to your journal and do some free or automatic writing with the card. Imagine the card is talking directly to you and giving you tips on how to open, use, and heal your third eye chakra center. Ask your card questions, and imagine it is speaking the answers to you. When you feel you have written all there is to write and can't seem to go any further by yourself, pick up your favorite tarot books and see what information you can gather about your selected card. Just keep the information relevant to the third eye, intuition, dreams, inner sight, outer sight, and future casting, which is a mix of NLP (neuro-linguistic programming) and spell work.

Once you have exhausted your research on your selected card, consider writing an affirmation or intention statement for this card to ground it. You don't have to do this, but I do recommend it, especially if the card you have selected represents something you are working toward or trying to create. This short affirmation or intention statement keeps you connected to your third eye chakra center while you heal, clear, and expand its power. Just take your time with the exercises, and allow your third eye significator to unfold information to you much the same way your third eye will. You will learn as you make your way through this chapter that sometimes your sight is clear, sometimes it is cloudy, and other times it locks you out completely. Energy doesn't just bend to our will. Instead, we learn to bend and to create with it. Let's dive deeper into the complex chakra known as the third eye.

· · · · ·

## 1. Intuition

This section could really be its own book, and there are plenty of stand-alone books on this topic. Some are really good, and some have missed the mark entirely. Some people really do understand the part the entire chakra system plays in intuition, while others really believe the third eye is its own island. By the time you have finished this small section on intuition, you will understand how this part of your vibrational being works together with all the other energy and collection points in your entire chakra system. Like it or not, you can't work on your intuition without working on everything else. Intuition is having the ability to understand something without conscious reasoning. It is a hunch, a feeling, a vibe, an instinct, a suspicion, an insight, or an impression, and many of these don't initially happen in the third eye—they happen in the lower chakras. They come together, however, in the third eye, oftentimes as an image, a puzzle piece, or an inner seeing. Our third eye may even be crucial to our survival, which means the root chakra plays a part in your intuition and has a vested interest in how you use it. As we learned back in chapter 1, our root chakra wants us to feel safe, secure, and stable. The third eye will alert us to concerns that the lower chakras have. Maybe this all happens automatically on an instinctual level, or perhaps it is learned behavior. My working theory is that it is a little of both, which would also mean we don't know as much about intuition as we would like to admit.

Intuition, like most things about humans as a species, is still something we have yet to fully understand, possibly because so few people have pushed the boundaries of what is possible with it. Like just about every other innate skill humans have, we seem happy to just work with it on the most basic of levels. We want it to perform party tricks and impress our friends. Yet intuition may very well be the final frontier of human biohacking and evolution. That is an exciting thought and something that is already being looked into by the Flow Genome Project, or "flow hackers," as they like to call themselves. They have partnered with Google to explore further how intuition may play a role in how we get into flow and how we tap into higher states of consciousness, thus enhancing our ability to think, heal, and problem-solve. In other words, some in the science community have moved intuition out of the spiritual and into the practical. I am personally thrilled by this sort of research as I believe everyone has a divine right to live to their fullest potential, whatever that means for them. These sorts of projects open doors to us finding out even more about who we are as individuals, as well as how intuition connects us as a species. This just brings us full circle to the idea that intuition is a full chakra experience, connected to both the earth we walk on and the vibrational universe from which we are constantly being reborn. It is an energy that runs through our entire body, impacting our own lives and the lives we share with others during each of our incarnations.

So how well is your intuition working?

## EXERCISE
· · · · ·

In order to find your current significator for this section, you will use only the major arcana cards from your deck. Hold them between the palms of your hands and take a few deep breaths, moving your focus to your third eye. If you need to, roll your eyes up as you breathe to help make the connection to your center of intuition. Rolling the eyes back down now, slowly shuffle the cards and then fan them out in front of you, keeping them face down. Close your eyes and take another few breaths before you scan the cards. Keeping your eyes closed, select the card that tingles, gives off a sensation to your fingers or hand, heats up, or feels cold. Turn it over so that the card is now face up. It is important that you keep this card in the orientation you drew it in, so if your card is reversed, keep it that way. If it is upright, keep it that way. This card is showing the current state of your intuition. Is it as good as you thought it was, or is it better?

Take your card to your journal and see how much you can write about this card in relation to intuition. Make sure you use words from this section, such as *hunch, instinct, impression, vibe, insight,* and *suspicion,* and write about how they work with the image of the card. When you have written all you can based on how the image makes you feel, pick up your favorite tarot books and see what else you can find out about your card. Look for words that we have used here to define intuition or acts of inner knowing. You might wish to build your intuition profile over a couple of days, which I highly recommend. Take your time and gather as much information as possible, as we are going to explore it further throughout this chapter.

· · · · ·

## 2. The Future

The third eye chakra, like the sacral and root chakras, is connected to time. The root chakra deals with the present, the sacral deals with the past, and here in the third eye, we get to delve into the future, or the possibility of a future. The third eye is where we hold the image of a future we want to create or where we get a glimpse of a future that is already unfolding before us. Time, as we know it, is a bit of a wonky construct, and the more we learn about quantum physics and quantum mechanics, the more we are realizing that time itself is not exactly a linear thing. This means that the past, present, and future may very well overlap and all influence each other, which is just another example of how the third eye works hand in hand with the lower chakras. Being able to see or hold a vision of the future is important not just in the law of attraction but also when it comes to healing work. You need to be able to see yourself in a state of well-being. You need to be able to hold an image of yourself recovering and being the person you always wanted to be. You need to be able to feel that image all the way through your vibrational core. This is how the third eye works to assist in reprogramming the lower chakras from a sick body to a healthy one. You have been practicing a bit of this already as you have been working through this book.

In the law of attraction, you learn to visualize with your third eye the life you want and the material things you desire. You imagine yourself having them, experiencing them, and engaging with them. The law states that if you do this often enough, you will no longer notice a separation between yourself and what you desire, and, therefore, your desires will end up showing up in your daily life. This is the third eye, the root, the sacral, and the solar plexus chakras all working together to bend time and space to create something that only you have been able to see inside your own head. It sounds like a magic trick, but we know that it is not. We have seen enough evidence of the law of attraction in action that we really cannot deny anymore that there is a web in the vibrational vortex that works in us and through us. This is great news for those on a healing path, as it means that you too can harness this time-bending power inside your chakras and move yourself into better and better states of well-being, with optimum health and wellness as your ultimate goal. You just have to be able to see it, hold that vision, and take action steps every day to make it a reality.

This begs the question, how good are you at imagining?

## EXERCISE
• • • •

Most people think that having an active imagination is for children, but that is not so. Our imaginations are the key to getting the third eye laser-focused on the future we are working to create. It is our imagination that allows us to see this future self happy, healthy, and loving life in the center of our third eye. It is imagination that engages the lower chakras and gets the whole wheel of vibrational attraction happening. This means in order for you to pick your future significator, you are going to have to fire up your imagination. Before you even pick up your cards, start imagining what your future healthy self looks and feels like.

Let your imagination run wild as it opens and engages your third eye. Is your future self pain-free or maybe anxiety-free? Is there a specific medical condition you are now seeing yourself free of in the future? Or maybe you can see yourself start to make improvements each and every day. This means having more and more days in health, but it will still be a work in progress. Whatever future you are focused on, just sit with it for a couple of minutes before you pick up your cards. Smile as you keep imagining and holding this future vision in your third eye, and show your body and your mind the joy this future brings you now, here in the present moment.

Once you feel happy, or even just at peace about the future you have seen with your inner sight, pick up your tarot cards and fan them out in front of you, face up. Search the cards for an image that comes close to the one you could see in your third eye. You more than likely won't find one exactly the same, but if you do, congratulations! What I really want you to look for is a card image that makes you feel similar to how you felt while you were seeing the healthy and happy future you. This means the card you are looking for gives off a vibration of peace and calm, happiness and joy, or even accomplishment and satisfaction. It really does depend on how you were feeling in your heart and your sacral. Now that you have selected your card, put it down in front of you and retrieve your significator card for the present and your significator card for the past. Line them up next to your future significator card. These three cards show how time is working in your chakra system. This sequence is unique to you and is aligned with your personal vibrational energy. Just know it is not fixed and can—and will—change as you get better and better at working with your entire chakra system. For now, examine the three cards you have before you.

```
┌─────┐  ┌─────┐  ┌─────┐
│     │  │     │  │     │
│  1  │  │  2  │  │  3  │
│     │  │     │  │     │
└─────┘  └─────┘  └─────┘
```

- *Card 1:* Future Significator
- *Card 2:* Present Significator ·
- *Card 3:* Past Significator

Take these cards to your journal and explore them. Write about how you imagine them working together. Create a story about these three cards and dig deep into the time-bending qualities they each have. Do as much freestyle writing as you can before you pick up your favorite tarot books and dig a little deeper. Remember to keep your research based on time, inner sight, imagination, and the future. If you want to take this one step further, you can create a vision board for your health and well-being and use it as a trigger for your third eye. Many of my healing clients have health and wellness vision boards to help them stay connected to their future self. It is not mixed with their bigger vision boards, and this one is smaller and very specific. If you wish to do the same, stay within the same parameters. Most importantly, have fun with this exercise, as that is kind of the point about imagining something that has yet to happen.

· · · · ·

## 3. Dreams

There are two types of dreams: the one you have at night when you go to sleep and the one you have about the possibilities for your life. Both of them happen here in the third eye. However, like most things that go on in this chakra center, they don't start here, but they finish here. Dreams are the end result of something else. The ones we have at night tend to come from one of two places. One is the leftover information of our day that has imprinted upon our heart, mind, and gut, and the other is the healing and clearing stirs of the past from the sacral chakra. Even nightmares are a way for the sacral to purge energy it feels needs to go. The dreams of our potential, the ones we have in private and rarely share with the world, come from the overlapping energies of the root, sacral, and heart chakras. If we ever take action on those dreams, we also start to engage the solar plexus and the throat.

As we become more confident about attaining our dreams, our crown chakra opens up more and more, yet the third eye does all the heavy lifting, as it is the one that has to hold the vision and steers the ship toward its destination. We explored this a little in the last section. Funny enough, the third eye doesn't know the difference between your awake dreams or asleep dreams. It just merely allows itself to be the screen on which they both shine.

The third eye believes the information must be important, as the lower chakras keep beaming it up. Therefore, it turns the dream or dreams into pictures, so you have a better understanding of the information that is pumping through your physical, mental, emotional, and vibrational bodies. The hilarious part of all of this is that most of us either don't remember our nighttime dreams or don't understand them. The third eye goes through all the trouble to help us out, and 90 percent of the time you just don't give it another thought—unless of course you are serious about dream journaling and studying your dreams is something you do on a regular basis.

The other dreams we have are connected to the future energy of the third eye chakra and its ability to see or hold an image of pretty much any future life we would like to experience. We all have these dreams, most often multiple times a day. We dream about travel, romance, money, health, and a million other things. While we do remember these dreams and have more control over them, just like our other dreams, only a small percentage of people take these dreams seriously. In fact, anything labeled a dream is either shrugged off or considered something that happens to other people, but dreams are powerful, and they can shape and reshape your life—only if you believe they are important. People give up on dreams every second of every day. As I sit here writing this chapter, thousands of people across the planet are giving up on something right now. All the hard work done by the third eye has been wasted.

Some dreams are easier to give up on than others. I give up on being my ideal body weight every time a piece of cake wanders into my line of sight! Some dreams we never let go of, even if they feel impossible. There is nothing worse than a life lived without ever seeing a big dream all the way through to the end. Your third eye chakra is already doing all the heavy lifting for you. It is holding the vision, and it keeps showing you what your life can look like. It is constantly giving you a visual map of how to achieve your dream, and yet despite all its efforts and all its late nights and early mornings, these dreams are often left unrealized.

However, I know you are different, because you are reading this book. You want to know how to heal and honor your third eye. You want to learn to work with your chakra system and not against it, which means you are willing to explore the vision your third eye has been holding for you. It believes in you, your lower chakras believe in you, and so do I. Just know this: the more we work toward our life dreams, the more whacked-out our night dreams can become. This is because your lower chakras are doing some serious cleaning, purging, and rearranging. Memories of past failures still circulating in the sacral may appear as warped and twisted nighttime dreams. This is all perfectly normal. See it as a triumph, and just keep doing the healing work in this book and with your coach or energy worker.

## EXERCISE
· · · · ·

To work with one's dreams, whether daytime or nighttime, is an act of bravery and courage. Keep this in mind as we move into pulling a significator for this section. This card should illustrate who you will be when you learn to master your dreams. Recommended cards for this significator include the High Priestess, the Hermit, Strength, the Hanged Man, the Tower, the Moon, the Knight of Cups, the Nine of Wands, the Eight of Swords, and the Seven of Pentacles.

Once you have selected your significator, journal with it for a while and see what sort of information you can get from your card. See if it has a dream story of its own to share with you. Just imagine it talking to you about your dreams, its dreams, and how they are intertwined. Just let the words flow, and don't try to make sense of them or even try to construct elegant sentences. The language of dreams very rarely makes sense, and dreams are often incoherent and tend to meander before really getting to the point. Just let your journal time with this card be free, and allow whatever needs to come up to come up. Once you have finished journaling with your card and you have explored your card's meaning further with your favorite tarot books, let's put it in a nice three-card spread so you can see how your dream energy works. You will need the birth and rebirth significator card from the sacral chakra, the self-expression card from the solar plexus chakra, and the card you just selected.

Lay them out as follows:

- *Card 1:* Birth and Rebirth Significator
- *Card 2:* Self-Expression Significator
- *Card 3:* Dreams Significator

These cards show you how the lower chakras are talking to your third eye. You have a creative birth in the sacral, which flares up to the solar plexus, where it decides how it wishes to be expressed in the world, and then it shoots up to the third eye to show you the finished outcome, that which the lower chakras have deemed possible. You might even want to take a picture of this spread, and keep it on your phone, so next time a lovely dream flashes across your third eye, you can remind yourself of the vibrational team that made this dream possible. Perhaps then you won't be so quick to dismiss it. Journal with this spread as well. Come up with your own dream story. Use these cards to assist you in becoming more confident about your dreams, both the healing aspects of your nighttime ones and your potentially life-changing daytime ones. Dreams are important, so don't be like everyone else and shrug them off. I have faith in you, and so do your chakras.

· · · · ·

## 4. Sight

The third eye chakra is in charge of our vision, through both our physical eyes and our inner eyes. We also have two parts of our brain that deal with sight as well, the visual field inside the primary motor cortex and the primary visual cortex in the occipital lobe. The physical eye bends light to create upside-down images, and it is the two corresponding parts of the brain that turn what we are seeing up the other way so that it makes sense for the visual, spatial world around us. Our natural vision is upside down, and that is how our eyes read light. Sometimes, that is how the third eye reads the messages from the lower chakras—in reverse. This is why so many people don't seem to understand or trust the visions they see with their inner eyes. They don't truly understand how they see. Sight and images are different things that work together in order for us to make a story around what we are seeing. We need light, logic, and imagination to be able to create images in the first place. In essence, sight is complex, and it requires lots of moving parts in both our body and our mind. However, most of us can see instantly through our physical eyes. For the most part, we take our eyes for granted, and we forget how entirely miraculous sight is. It explains why people get frustrated with developing and growing their inner sight, as they expect it to work as seamlessly as seeing their own physical eyes, which, with some time and understanding, it can. However, unlike your physical sight, your inner sight needs you to understand how it works and how it puts together vibrational energy from the lower chakras and draws them up to the third eye to make images that your brain can see and understand.

## EXERCISE
· · · · ·

In the section on intuition, I discussed how the lower chakras send important pieces of information to the third eye, information that the vibrational body feels you really need to know about. Just like the light that comes into the physical eyes, this information more often than not comes in upside down, which is why working with reversed tarot cards can help you develop your intuitive sight, and this is why the significator card for this section will be a reversed card. Grab your tarot deck and find a card that you think best represents inner sight. Recommended cards for this are the High Priestess, the Hanged Man, Justice, the Tower, the Moon, the Ace of Cups, the Ace of Swords, the Eight of Swords, the Two of Swords, the Nine of Cups, and any of the cups court cards.

Once you have your card selected, turn it upside down and keep it upside down. Do not be tempted to turn it around just because the logical part of your brain wants everything to be in some sort of order. Notice what happens when you turn the card upside down. What was at the bottom is now at the top, and what was at the top is now at the bottom. In your journal, write about how changing the order of things changes how you react to the image, especially if you went from a point of understanding to a point of confusion. Keep in mind that both your physical eyes and your third eye are more than capable of reading and understanding images and information, regardless of the order they are in, so try not to think too hard as you write about this card. Consider using sentence starters like "I see that the sky is now..." or "The first thing I see is..." You may even say, "I can see this card as if it were..." By including "I see" statements, you are affirming that you are using your sight rather than your brain. It is important to keep affirming what you see and not what you think. You can even make a list in your journal of all the things you see on the card. This will also help you pick out identifiable information, even if it doesn't seem like it is in the correct or logical order. This is how to connect what you see to what you know. When you do this, you get understanding, but you need to know what you are seeing in order to understand it.

When you have finished journaling with this card, just place it in front of you, keeping it upside down. Take a couple of nice, deep breaths, and imagine an indigo smoky light coming out of your third eye chakra. As you exhale, the indigo smoky light grows and starts to wrap its tendrils around you and the card in front of you. Imagine this smoky light infusing the card, lighting it up, and making it appear to glow. Take another nice, deep breath, pick up your deck, and begin to shuffle slowly. Watch the indigo smoky light come from your hands and merge with the deck in between your palms. Once you feel the deck is infused with the energy from your third eye chakra, just hold the cards between your hands for a moment and ask the following questions:

1. What am I not seeing?

2. What do I need to see?

3. What should I stop looking at?

Draw a card for each of these questions and lay your spread out as illustrated below:

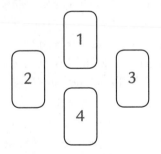

- *Card 1:* Sight Significator
- *Card 2:* What am I not seeing?
- *Card 3:* What do I need to see?
- *Card 4:* What should I stop looking at?

Keep the cards you pulled in the orientation you pulled them, meaning if you pulled the cards in the upright aspect, keep them that way. If you pulled them upside down, keep them that way. This spread gives you some clues to how your current sight, both internally and externally, is doing. Where your focus should be and where it is are always very telling of what sort of energy we allow to dominate our vision. Keep in mind that what you are not seeing refers to things already in your line of sight, whereas what you need to see is something you aren't even focused on because you have your attention on what you need to stop looking at. The longer you sit with this spread, the more connectors you will find. You might even find that what you are not seeing in your current experience is directly connected to where your sight should be focused. This includes missed opportunities for healing or better understanding your third eye chakra. This spread is very useful to do when you feel stuck, at a crossroads, or blocked. Take your time working with each of the cards in this spread. Dig as deep as you want to. Explore them on a literal and symbolic level. The more information you have, the more you can heal and engage your third eye chakra.

· · · · ·

## 5. Perception

Perception, or how you see things, is how you live your life. Everything you do, say, or believe is based on your perception of the information you are constantly receiving from the outside world. Perception even shapes who you see yourself to be and the part you think you are here to play. Perception rules our lives. It will limit us or liberate us. It will allow us to exceed our wildest dreams, or it will keep us living small, sad, and regret-based lives. The best part about perception, however, is that it is not solid. It is not set in stone, and it is constantly changing.

Perception starts and ends in the third eye chakra, but it involves the entire chakra system. You could call it the classic glass half-full or half-empty way of looking at life. Some people's perception is set to see only what is missing, while others see only what they have to be grateful for. Some will either be constantly complaining about everything wrong with their life, or they will be constantly raving on about the blessings of their life. This is how you tell how your perception is set. Listen to yourself speak about your life. I truly need you to understand how impactful your lens of perception is. The way you look at the world, the way you see the things in the world, and the way you visualize yourself in that world sets the tone for every single aspect of your existence.

The information you receive, the opportunities you create, the money you make, the relationships you have—all of this is viewed and attracted through your lens of perception. However, it is a lens you can change at any time. In healing work, we use perception to move people out of their illness stories, because if someone is constantly seeing themselves as ill and saying they are ill, it is very hard to align with health. In order for healing to take place, you have to see yourself differently, and you have to shift that lens of perception all the time. You might start by changing "I am a person with chronic illness" to "I am healing from chronic illness." Then you will shift to "I am in the process of healing," to "I am healed," and then to "I am healthy." With each shift, you claim a new identity and construct a new narrative for your life, but you do it by seeing yourself differently, holding that vision of yourself, and allowing your lens of perception to shape the world around you to fit your new vision. By doing this sort of slow and gradual perception work with my clients, I have seen them go from chronic illness to rapid recovery times and getting on with life in under a year. The only thing we really did was change their perception, shift what they saw, and move that new vision up and through the chakras.

## EXERCISE
· · · · ·

Because your lens of perception is so important, really take your time picking your ideal significator card for this section. It is crucial you don't get Pollyanna about this center of vision in the third eye. Wanting to see things in a way they can't possibly be is just as limiting and harmful as seeing lack everywhere. A healthy lens of perception allows people, places, and things to just be what they are. The only thing you are changing is how you wish to view them. For example, we can't change difficult people, but we can see them as people carrying around a lot of old wounds rather than people who want to make us miserable. We also can't change other people's paths, but we can see them being exactly where they are meant to be, based on their own lens of perception, and accept them for where they are, rather than where we would prefer them to be. You are really looking for a card that echoes how you want to see yourself and the world around you. Recommended cards are the Sun, Temperance, the Hierophant, the Empress, the Wheel of Fortune, Judgement, any of the aces, the Three of Pentacles, the Four of Wands, the Three of Cups, and the Eight of Swords.

Once you have selected your card, open your journal and write about what the world would look like through the perception of the card you have chosen. Imagine yourself as the card you have chosen and write about what you see, how you see it, and what feelings you have about wearing this card as a new skin. Get as descriptive as you can in this journal exercise, as you have deliberately chosen this card for a reason. Dig deep, and just let the words come to you without thinking too much about them. Just remember you are not writing something that is going to be judged; it does not have to be perfect, and each word does not need to be precisely added. Just let the words out as they come. It doesn't even matter if for now it doesn't even make sense. Your writing might come as a list, short sentences, a paragraph or two, or a complete page. It matters not. What is important is doing the exercise and allowing yourself to explore this new shift in perception. When you feel you have dumped as much as you can onto the page, pick up your deck and draw a card for the following question:

*What action step can I take right now to shift my perception into a more positive state?*

Place this card next to your perception significator and imagine them having a conversation. This dialogue between the cards could bring up some key answers to the above question. Pick up your pen and see if you can transcribe some of this exchange between the two cards. Don't worry about grammar or spelling or even trying to make sentences. Just write down what you perceive or imagine yourself hearing. You can always explore it more deeply in your journal at some other time. Keep the conversation going between the two cards until you feel it has come to an end, and if you want to, see if you can pull anything out of what you have written that might be explored further. If you feel now is not the time, you can always do it later. Perception shifts slowly, each day, over time, so you can't rush this, but you can commit to making that shift each and every day by checking in with where you are and seeing what steps you can take to get you to where you want to be.

· · · · ·

## 6. Bias

Whether we like to admit it or not, we all view the world through bias. This bias comes from our beliefs and alters our point of perception. Bias also filters the information that comes our way and decides what we will be interested in and what we won't. Bias has a way of blocking our potential, as it works to limit our exposure to opportunities, people, and information. When we only look out for things that we prefer based on what we have experienced in the past, we can miss some amazing points of growth. Bias can, and does, interfere with one's healing journey, as people often tend to stick to things they feel comfortable with rather than seek out things that could actually get them results. Bias also filters what you see and what you allow yourself to see with your third eye. You will tend to focus only on images, visions and flashes of inspiration that you are partial too. One of the biggest mistakes people make about bias is that they tend to think it only applies to insidious aspects of life, like being biased against a race of people or a religion, but this is just not true. We have bias toward everything: flowers, pets, color and styles of clothes, footwear, the food we eat, the music we listen to, and the movies and television shows we watch. Bias simply means we are either for something or against it. Bias decides what goes in our pro column and what goes in the con column. It is a very simple concept that has a massive impact on how we move through the world.

Bias, like perception, is a lens. It's a way of seeing the world, ourselves, and everyone in it. It is how we order that world and give it structure and meaning. It is also how we sort our place in it. We decide if we are better or worse than other sentient beings and ascribe a pecking order and slot ourselves in. Once we have figured out where we are in the world order, we use that bias to keep us there. The third eye chakra, however, doesn't work with bias in the same way as the mind, and this is where the trouble starts to arise. Inspiration knows no order or hierarchy; rather it just knows information and vibration, so it sends something important your way only to have it screened once by your perception and then again by your bias. By the time you start paying attention to your third eye, the information you get is a watered-down version of what it originally was. This happens to all of us. The only difference is that some people are aware of bias at work and question everything, especially what shows up in the third eye. In other words, we are all slowly unraveling our bias and perception out of the information and allowing it to stand on its own merit without interference from us.

Keep in mind that your third eye chakra is not an island. It works hand in hand with the entire chakra system, so bias here is bias that flows all the way through you. That's a lot of unraveling that needs to happen in order for us to get to the truth of our health, well-being, and overall happiness. Bias is not something we ever get rid of. We are always going to have likes, dislikes, and preferences, and that's just part of being human. This energy is always going to be the lens we see through. We can, however, shift them, become aware of them, and learn to question our way around them. In other words, we can become a better steward or caregiver for our bias.

## EXERCISE
· · · · ·

What sort of steward or caregiver do you wish to be for your bias in the third eye chakra? How will you stand guard against your bias, as it arises in this energy center? Think about these two questions for a while before you consider deliberately selecting a significator for this section. You will need to have a steward who is not only vigilant but fair, who understands not all bias is bad, and who will be committed to helping you clean and clear this energy so that you can see with better clarity. Recommended cards for this significator are Strength; the Tower; the Devil; Justice; Judgement; the Knight, Queen, and King of Swords; the Two of Swords; the Eight of Swords; and the Knight, Queen, and King of Wands.

Once you have selected your significator, take it to your journal and start asking it some questions. Start with this: "How is my current bias sabotaging my healing journey?" Be open to the answer to this question. Don't try to make it pretty or elegant, but just let the answer come up, and then use that answer to ask another question. For example, perhaps the message of your card is food or money. Ask how your bias toward these things is getting in the way of your health. Whatever the answer appears to be, use that to ask another question.

Between each question, give yourself a moment to connect with your third eye. Ask your question, close your physical eyes, and allow what you see and what you hear to help answer your question. You may find images will start to pop up each time you question something, as if each question becomes a trigger. This is good, and this means you are allowing your third eye chakra to join in the conversation. If you find nothing is coming up or the images are more flashes of color or light, that is good also. It just means you are starting the dialogue process with your third eye. Don't give up—just keep going. Do this Q and A session with your significator card until you run out of questions. Then go back over your answers and see what sort of information you have uncovered.

Don't be discouraged if your session is short or you feel like you didn't get a lot of words on the page. Just keep doing the healing and clearing work, and it will all come with time, patience, and practice. If, however, you feel you need additional information about the answers you received, pull a card or two, lay them next to your significator, and see if that helps round things out. The more you understand how bias is working in your third eye, the more you will be able to see how it is impacting your day-to-day life. Each baby step is progress in your healing work. Just keep going.

· · · · ·

## 7. Clarity

Along with intuition, clarity is the main reason most people wish to develop their third eye chakra, as a healthy functioning third eye means clear vision. When we have clear vision, we have less doubt and therefore can make decisions more efficiently. It is an admirable thing to want to be consistently crystal clear about what you see, what your intuition is telling you, and what messages your body is sending you. Just know that you can also have perfect clarity and still do nothing. You can see through your lens of bias, move around your perception, and still stay in the same place. Clarity can also increase anxiety and unsettle the root chakra, making you feel under threat. Clarity isn't just about being able to see things more clearly; it is also about being able to comprehend things at a deeper level. It is about understanding and a knowingness that rings so true it cannot be denied. Understanding is an act of acceptance. When we understand something, we accept it for what it is. With clarity comes the knowledge that what you are seeing is what you are seeing. When something is crystal clear, you can no longer deny it, and you are not always seeing things that will bring you joy or gaining clarity on things you want to experience. In other words, clarity doesn't only bring good news with it, and this may be one reason you struggle to open and surrender to the energy of your third eye chakra.

It is also why we don't work with the third eye like it's an island. It is part of a much larger energy system, and in order for us to truly be able to get clear, commit to our healing journey, and not be afraid of what we hear, speak, and see, we need our lower chakras happy and healthy. It is the reaction your lower chakras make to what you see that will either move you into even deep clarity or make you want to shut down and block your third eye chakra. Blocking the third eye chakra is not something we want to do, as this blocks energy from reaching up from the lower chakras to the crown chakra, and it blocks energy coming down from the crown chakra to the lower chakras.

So how does one step into clarity, but not run away in fear, when they start seeing things that trigger them? The answer is to do it slowly and by gently breathing into the moment. We don't have to like what clarity brings us, but we do need to sit with it to get a better understanding of the information. The only way to really do that is to gently and lovingly breathe into it.

## EXERCISE
· · · · ·

How do you see yourself as the master of your clarity and as the person who can, slowly and gently, breathe in new information, regardless of whether you judge it to be good or bad? Pick up your deck and search for a card that you feel is the best representation of the clear and concise person you wish to be. This significator is courageous, strong, and gentle, yet it craves understanding. Recommended cards are the Hierophant, Strength, the Hermit, Temperance, Justice, Judgement, and any of the queens.

Once you have chosen your significator card, just place it face up in front of you, and place your hands over it. Take a nice, deep breath and relax your shoulders. Take another nice, deep breath, this time through your heart, and focus that breath in and out of your heart chakra. As you gently breathe in and out through the heart space, image a deep indigo light shining at your third eye point in the middle of your brow. With each breath in and out of your heart, this light becomes a deeper and deeper indigo color, while it very slowly expands in size. Don't try to force the third eye. Just let it gently do its own thing while you stay connected to the breath and your heart chakra. Just allow yourself to settle into having these two chakras open and working in tandem, keeping your hand on your card, as you create this energy loop for your center of clarity.

When you are relaxed and not resisting this energy loop, repeat this sentence: "I willingly accept clarity in all areas of my life." Say this statement aloud three times. Once you are done, take a deep breath in through the nose and out through the mouth and then another in the same way, letting the heart chakra and third eye, slowly and gently, reduce in size and disconnect from the loop. Take one more breath in through the nose and out through the mouth, and remove your hand from the card, bringing your awareness back to the room and back into your body.

Now take your card to your journal. Write about the experience you just had, while making a connection to your card, your third eye, and your heart. Discuss anything that may have come up or that you saw during the connection loop. Perhaps you noticed something in your physical body, such as a pain, tingling, or nausea. If anything happened, write it down. Consider starting your journal session with this sentence: "As I begin to accept my vision and open my center of clarity, I notice that ..." Go ahead and finish that sentence off with anything that popped up for you. Some of what you experienced will be resistance, and this could even be in the form of "I don't like fill-in-the-blank exercises." Some of it will also be acceptance. It is the acceptance you are looking to increase, as this is what you will need to assist you on your healing journey. It is only when we accept what is that we can then move into creating something new. Think of it this way: when you can see clearly and accept what is right in front of you, you can then make a plan to move around it and forge ahead with clarity of purpose.

· · · · ·

## Third Eye Chakra Tarot Healing

Now that you have worked through the seven key issues of the sixth chakra, it is time to do some energy healing work on all that you have discovered, all that has bubbled up, and all that has presented itself for cleaning and clearing. Grab your tarot deck and get out the significator cards for the issues covered in this chapter. Select your significator card for the third eye chakra and place it in front of you. This card is going to be the middle card in your third eye chakra healing mandala wheel.

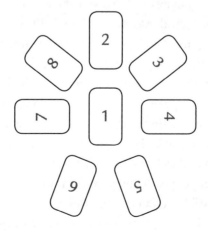

Your card order is as follows:

- *Card 1:* Third Eye Chakra Significator
- *Card 2:* Intuition Significator
- *Card 3:* Future Significator
- *Card 4:* Dreams Significator
- *Card 5:* Sight Significator
- *Card 6:* Perception Significator
- *Card 7:* Bias Significator
- *Card 8:* Clarity Significator

Your center card is going to be the energy you will see flowing in and out of the other cards, as if a beautiful indigo smoke wisps out of the card and starts to tickle the other cards around it. As we move into the visualization part of this exercise, move your hands over the cards as you say the following affirmations for each of the cards surrounding your third eye chakra significator. The tarot mandala helps anchor your energy healing work and allows you to engage more fully with the overall process. Your affirmations are as follows:

- *Card 2:* I am naturally intuitive.
- *Card 3:* I am able to hold a vision for my future without attachment.
- *Card 4:* I am allowing myself to dream as big as the universe.
- *Card 5:* I am trusting what I see in both my physical and inner eyes.
- *Card 6:* I am able to question my lens of perception.

- *Card 7:* I am being very aware of my personal bias.
- *Card 8:* I am giving myself permission to accept clarity.

Find somewhere comfortable and quiet where you won't be disturbed for up to twenty minutes. Place your cards where you can see them and start rubbing your palms gently together as you focus on your breathing. Rub your hands together for about forty seconds, activating the energy centers in your palms. You might start to feel some heat in your hands, and this is good. Now place your hands over your third eye point or brow and focus on your breath, inhaling through your nose. Feel the breath as it hits the back of your throat, fills your lungs, and expands your chest. As you exhale from the mouth, feel the breath leaving your body and deflating the lungs. Let the breath work become automatic, and shift your focus to your cards, starting with the center card, which is your third eye chakra significator. Visualize the indigo smoke gently rising from the card and twirling around the wheel you have created around it. Each time you exhale, the smoky wisps extend farther and farther. Sit like this for a few minutes, just doing the breath work and keeping your hands on your brow area as you feel your chest rise and fall, and visualize the smoky indigo energy infusing your spread.

When you feel ready, move your hands to your tarot mandala and move them along each card as you speak the corresponding affirmation statements out loud. Read through the entire list three times. Once you have finished, just relax and focus on the breath work, placing the hands back over your brow. As you inhale, feel the smoky indigo energy coming into your nose, sending it up to the brow point and infusing the third eye chakra. Relax into this, as you inhale all this lovely infused energy, letting it clean and clear your third eye chakra as it embeds your affirmations into your chakra. When this feels complete, remove your hands and just breathe normally for thirty to forty seconds. Thank your cards, and you are done.

You can repeat this simple tarot healing session anytime you want, and by all means, journal about how the session made you feel or any revelations you had during the session. The more you know, the more you inquire, the more you heal.

# The Crown Chakra

The crown chakra is located at the very top of your head (hence why it is called the crown), and it is the first part of yourself that is pushed through the womb—unless, of course, you were born feet first. Generally speaking, once crowning happens during the birth process, the baby is ready to come bursting forth into the world, crown chakra wide open and exposed for all to see. The crown chakra is our point of connection to what some call the Divine, but you could also call it our connector to the vibrational world. The root connects us to the physical realm, and the crown connects us to the vibrational world. One reminds us of where we have come from, and the other reminds us of where we are. We are plugged into two worlds at the same time, vibrational (or energetic) and physical. Inside this chapter, you are going to explore seven issues the crown chakra deals with on a consistent and ongoing basis. These seven issues each have their own section in this chapter, as they all have important information for you regarding the health and well-being of your crown chakra.

The sections are as follows:

1. Connection

2. Divinity

3. Wholeness

4. Awareness

5. Wisdom

6. Potential

7. Inspiration

## Sahasrara

The crown chakra, or *sahasrara*, as it is known in Sanskrit, is in charge of the rest of the head, especially the brain, which, just like the crown, is not fully understood. We know so little about how the human brain works, though science is picking up speed in its studies. We also know very little about what the crown chakra actually does. This also means we haven't really explored how the energy that is pumped from the universe or the Divine through our crown into our bodies could truly change our lives and the world at large. This is pretty exciting, as I would hate to think we have become all we could possibly be.

The crown chakra works in tandem with all the chakras underneath it, and it comes into its full power when the lower chakras are open, healthy, and functioning unencumbered. The more constricted, blocked, torn, or sluggish your lower chakras are, the more the crown will struggle and the more you will doubt your place and purpose in the physical world. The crown chakra is your center of awareness as well as your center of potential, and in order to grow and expand, you need your crown chakra open and spinning. You need to have some control over your entire chakra system in order to tap into the power of your crown. Just remember we still don't really know how powerful a fully functioning crown chakra, with an amped up chakra system, can be. Even in monastic circles, such as the Thai Buddhism my wife studies, monks talk about the many levels of awareness that lie beyond the awakening or enlightened portal. The monk my wife trains under is constantly telling her that waking up is only step one. Awakening is merely unlocking the next level of the crown chakra. How many levels lie beyond that we truly don't know.

The crown chakra also deals with our relationship to a higher power. You may call it God, the universe, the Goddess, or your higher self, and truly, the label is irrelevant. It is our belief and relationship to something beyond our physical existence. If you have a troubled or complicated relationship with this energy, you will also have a complicated relationship with your crown chakra. I put myself into the camp of complicated relationships, and I am very aware of how this complicated, sticky relationship I have with the unknown affects my physical experience. Some people are just incredibly trusting in what they can't see. They easily hand things off to a higher power all the time, with no doubt that what needs to be taken care of will be. There are others who are certain that nothing beyond what they can see, feel, touch, taste, and smell exists; that we are alone; and that when we die, we will cease to exist. You could say that the crown chakra is our center of faith. Some of us have it, some of us wrestle with it, and some of us don't have any at all.

## EXERCISE

· · · · ·

What is your relationship with your crown chakra like?

You are about to find out as you pull your significator card. You are going to pull this card intuitively and only from the major arcana cards, so go ahead and separate them out of your deck now. Give them a quick shuffle and fan them out in front of you face down. Sit back for a moment, place your hands over your heart chakra, and take a couple of nice, deep, centering breaths. Next, imagine a golden light, like a beam of sunlight, shining onto the top of your head. Feel it as it moves down your arms and into your hands. Place your hands just above the fanned-out cards in front of you without touching them, and imagine this lovely golden sunlight hitting just one of the cards. You see this light dance over the card, giving off a glow. Turn the card over so you can see it, and take three nice, deep breaths, slowly letting the golden light leave your imagination and bringing your awareness back to the room and back to your body.

Put the other cards back into your tarot deck and take the card your crown chakra selected to your journal. Start your journal session by describing the card in as much detail as possible. Then, move into discussing how the card makes you feel. Underline any intense or uncomfortable feelings that arise. They may end up becoming important as you move through this chapter. Finish up your journal writing by referring to your favorite tarot books for further meaning and deeper understanding around your crown chakra significator card. Now that you and your crown have started a dialogue, let's continue it throughout the rest of this chapter.

• • • • •

## 1. Connection

Our energetic body has two massive power points at each end, one at the root chakra and one at the crown chakra. One plugs us into the physical world so we can have a physical experience, and the other plugs us into the vibrational world so we have access to the energy from which we came. Being plugged in at both ends means we have a well-functioning energy body, one in which our chakras are spinning happily and we have a steady mix of earthly and cosmic energy running through us. This makes us feel connected, whole, courageous, confident, and at home in our skin. When our crown chakra is blocked or having trouble connecting into the energy of the universe/God/Goddess, we feel isolated, alone, aimless, and paranoid. This is because half of our vital life energy is not pumping through our bodies.

In many respects, the energy of the root chakra is echoed here in the crown. When one is not connected, the rest of the chakra system struggles, and so do we. In the root chakra, we need connection to help us feel like we belong in the physical world, but here in the crown, that sense of belonging is bigger than the material world. It is the need to belong to something larger than ourselves. At the crown chakra, what we are really seeking is a connection to home, to the place we came from and the place we shall return once we have slipped out of our physical robe. Our crown chakra is our cosmic grounding point, whereas the root is our material and matter grounding point, each establishing our purpose for being.

## EXERCISE
· · · · ·

You may have heard someone say, "I want to feel connected to something bigger than myself," "I want to do something bigger with my life," or even, "I don't know what my purpose is." These are all crown chakra statements. They require a need to be plugged in and connected to the cosmic energy that extends beyond the limitations of the physical world. This is the crown chakra needing to burst open, wanting desperately to reconnect to the energy that bought it into existence in the first place. You might have even uttered these statements once or twice yourself. In fact, there is a good chance you are having a crown chakra moment in your life right now. I mean, you are reading this book!

Pick up your tarot deck and give it a shuffle. Then, pull a card to answer each of the following questions:

- *Card 1:* How connected am I to my purpose?
- *Card 2:* When I think about living a bigger, bolder life, what message do I send to my crown chakra?
- *Card 3:* What makes me block my crown chakra?
- *Card 4:* When I am feeling disconnected, what action can I take to plug back in?

These four cards will give you a snapshot of what is going on with your crown chakra right now. Just remember these cards can, and do, change as you continue to heal, clear, and trust in your crown's connective energy. For now, they give you a good idea of how open or closed your top power connecter is. These cards may also give you a hint to which lower chakras are causing problems here in the crown:

- *Pentacles:* Earth = root
- *Cups:* Water = sacral
- *Swords:* Air = heart
- *Wands:* Fire = solar plexus

Take these cards and their lower chakra correspondences to your journal, and spend some time writing about how these energies are either enhancing or impacting your crown chakra's ability to connect to universal/God/Goddess energy. Remember, these cards are answers to specific questions, so consider starting your writing as if you are reporting findings about your questions. Think about something like this: "My current connection energy to my purpose is…" or "Whenever I think about making big, bolder changes in my life, my crown acts like…" or "When I feel disconnected, I can tap back in by using the…" Write for as long as you can, just off the top of your head, as it is important you build a personal relationship with each of your cards in relation to the chakra you are working with. When you feel you have exhausted your own knowledge, grab your trusted tarot books and search for key words or phrases that align to your findings.

Once you have finished with your findings and your journal work, it is time to select a connection significator card. If the four question cards did not show up as favorable or showed you have some work to do to get this energy where it needs to be, think about finding a card that is the ideal for your point of connection or a card that you will aspire to become. If the four question cards filled you with joy and showed you are indeed working on that power of connection, then look for a card that you feel you already embody but still have room to grow with, because—let's face it—there is always room for improvement, no matter where we are. Recommended cards for your connection significator are the Queen of Swords, the Fool, the Empress, Temperance, the Star, and any of the aces.

Once you have your significator card, place it with the four answer cards you just pulled and make this into a spread. Lay the cards out as follows:

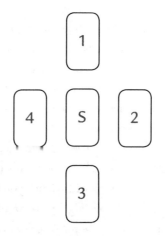

Now that you have your cards all laid out, you can see how your connection energy is moving and flowing. Is there anything that stands out to you now that you have the significator card in the middle that you did not see when you were just journaling with the cards separately? Grab your journal and write any new findings you have about your connection energy, now that you have a complete spread to work from. Consider working with this spread first up and down and then left to right. See how breaking them up into two card lines changes the information they give. Take your time and have fun with these cards. Explore their messages and information with an open heart and an open mind.

· · · · ·

## 2. Divinity

Divinity is our divine nature. It is the holy and blessed part of who we are. Our center of divinity at the crown chakra deals with not only our personal divinity but also divinity in others and how we see divine energy in our lives. It really is our God or Goddess center, showing how we see ourselves as a reflection of God or the Goddess, how we define our relationship with God or the Goddess, and how we see God or the Goddess reflected in others. If we have a complicated relationship with God/the Goddess/the Divine, we will have a complicated relationship with all aspects of divinity.

I should point out that I am not talking about religion. Religion has nothing to do with divinity or our relationship to God, the Goddess, and divine energy. One does not need to be religious to have a healthy, joyous, and expansive relationship with divinity or the Divine. When we talk about the Divine or God or the Goddess, we are simply talking about a higher power. This higher power is both us and something else, and it is an energy that creates miracles, such as miracles like you and me. Our center of divinity deals in unwavering faith, faith in ourselves, faith in others, and faith in the universe at large. People with a good grasp on their divinity never question how things will work out, and they are always expecting miracles to show up in their daily lives. They believe in a larger divine plan for themselves and humanity. These people walk a path of deep and profound faith. I admire this type of person greatly, as I'm not one of them. My relationship to divinity is complicated, and yours might be as well. This is perfectly fine, as long as you know and accept your current relationship status, for now you have room to heal and grow.

Why is this important? Why do we need to be concerned with divinity, and what does it have to do with healing? One of the things I have noticed in the decade I have been working with clients is that those who have a clear, albeit imperfect, connection to divinity are more likely to be committed to healing work. They understand they are meant to be here, in this physical life, for a reason, and they feel a pull for themselves to move out of illness and into health and well-being so they can show up more completely in their own lives. Those who do not have a connection to divinity or have blocked their center of divinity find it much harder to let go of their illness stories. They can't move beyond their pain and suffering because they don't see a reason to. These clients tend to drop out of the healing journey quickly. This is why divinity is important to your healing journey. You need to feel that connection to the higher power inside yourself and outside yourself. You need to feel the pull to something bigger, brighter, and joyous that only divine energy can bring to your experience, for when you understand you are divine and that divine energy is your energy, you understand your true nature.

## EXERCISE
· · · · ·

Now it is time to deliberately select your significator for divinity. This card will embrace your version of what you think your divine self looks and feels like. Try to imagine yourself as someone who is in the flow of divine energy, meaning you feel it all around you and have faith that it is always available to you, even if right this second you don't believe it to be true. See yourself glowing with golden light. Watch as the golden light shoots from your fingers and toes, making you appear like a star covered in pixie dust. When you can see this version of yourself clearly, pick up your deck of tarot cards and search the images until you find your significator. Recommended cards include the Hierophant, Strength, the

Hermit, the Tower, the Star, Judgement, any of the aces, any of the knights, and any of the kings.

Once you have your significator card, take it to your journal and spend some time getting to know it in relation to divine energy. Keep in mind everything you write or read about this card now has to be in alignment with the purpose you have given it, which in this case is divinity. What does this card tell you about your divine self, and how can it help you stay connected to the divine energy of those around you? You may wish to answer this question by listing the divine aspects of your card, the divine aspects in yourself, and then the divine aspects of those around you. If nothing else, this will expand your awareness of where divinity is in your life and give you some nice key words, such as *blessed, grace, flow, miracle, light, radiant,* and *peaceful,* to explore further in your journal writing.

When you feel you have explored your card as much as you can in this initial sitting, let's move on to a quick three-card spread to see how this energy of divinity plays with some of your other chakra centers. The two additional cards needed for this spread are your significator card for fellowship and your significator card for engagement. Lay them out as follows:

- *Card 1:* Divinity Significator
- *Card 2:* Fellowship Significator
- *Card 3:* Engagement Significator

Now pick up your remaining cards and slowly shuffle the deck, imagining a golden light flowing out of your hands and into the cards. When the cards feel infused, draw three cards and lay them directly under your three significator cards. Now you will have six cards in total laid out before you in two rows of three. The first row is the ideal flow of energy from one chakra to the next, and the second row is the current flow of energy from one chakra to the next. Is there a big difference between the cards you pulled in the second row and the significators in the top row, or does it look similar but slightly different? Write your findings in your journal. Start by comparing the two spreads, then move on to comparing and dialoguing with the individual cards. Do this by pairing up the two divinity cards, then the two fellowship cards, and then the two engagement cards. There will be an incredible amount of information for you to wade through, so take your time while you listen, explore, and make notes on possible points of healing.

· · · · ·

## 3. Wholeness

For the most part, people seek wholeness in the world of physicality, other people, and material things. The idea of twin flames and soul mates was born from the idea that somewhere there is another piece of you striving to find you, and that once these two halves find each other they can both be whole once again. These stories have been twisted and distorted by their retelling over the years, which makes them as reliable as any other message that took over a thousand people to tell it before it reached you. This idea that something or someone else in the physical world can make us feel whole is a lie, a con, and a fabulous sales pitch. The truth is the piece of ourselves we are seeking is the larger part of ourselves that can't fit inside our physical form, as it is too big to cram into our little human bodies. It is what some would call the higher self, though, to be honest, labeling it is not really that important. People will spend tens of thousands of dollars trying to make themselves whole, just as they will actively spend thousands of hours seeking the feeling of being whole with people and things. But the truth is this feeling that we all crave can't be bought, nor can someone else give it to us, because it can't be found outside the self. It is something that happens here inside the crown chakra and is an energy we are connected to, which we then send to the heart and then to the root. This energy, once it is sent back down the lower chakras, makes us feel whole, complete, and at one with ourselves and the world around us.

The crown chakra plugs into the vibrational energy of the universe, and yes, that does sound vast, overwhelming, and sometimes terrifying. This feeling of being plugged into something so immense can initially make you feel small and insignificant, and it is at this point most people disconnect and forget all about trying to work with the energy of the crown. However, if you keep at it and sit with that energy long enough, you will stop feeling overwhelmed and instead start to feel whole, compete, and at home. It is important to give yourself time to get used to the energy that is pumping through your crown, as it is not like the more contained energy you are used to. The higher self knows no limits, and it is never contained. This also means it can feel powerful, wild, and out of control. For all the control freaks of the world, this feeling is not comfortable at all, and initially you will reject it. Let's face it, we have a better chance of controlling our shopping, our lovers, our friends, and our family than we do the universe, so we stick to finding other, more controllable things to make us feel something that only being tapped into our higher selves truly can.

## EXERCISE
· · · · ·

Wholeness is a courageous act. It requires us to be vulnerable and to accept what we don't know and what we can't control. Becoming one with yourself will be the bravest thing you ever do, which is why it is important to deliberately find a significator card that makes you feel confident and strong but also vulnerable, and maybe even a little shaky in the knees. Recommended cards for this significator are the Lovers, Strength, Temperance, the Sun, the Two of Cups, the Four of Wands, the Seven of Wands, the Eight of Swords, the Seven of Pentacles, and any of the pages.

Once you have selected your significator, take it to your journal and start by imagining this card as yourself as you stand before the vastness of the universe. Allow the fears to bubble up first, and imagine telling yourself all the things that scare you about tapping into something so big and powerful and uncontrollable. You can write this out as a dialogue or just make a list. How you write it is not as important as getting it onto paper. When you feel you have gotten everything on your list, it is time to ask your card self what the benefits of feeling whole are and how it would change your life if you suddenly felt complete and comfortable in your skin all the time? Again, you can write this as a dialogue or a list.

Now that you have completed your conversation or complied two lists, you can do a bit of a compare and contrast against your fears and your benefits. One list will have more weight and pull to it than the other, and that list is the one you are currently allowing to dictate the terms of your crown chakra energy. If you want to take it a step further, lay the following cards out:

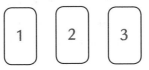

- *Card 1:* Wholeness Significator
- *Card 2:* Safety Significator
- *Card 3:* Decision-Making Significator

These three cards give you a visual of how your energy is when you feel like you have everything you need, feel safe in your skin, and are confident about your ability to make decisions. When we feel we are whole, we feel safe to make bolder decisions. We don't need to keep our lives or our dreams small. Instead, we free ourselves up to imagine a life that is larger than life. We become brave, courageous, and, above all, at peace with who we are, why we are here, and our place not just in the world, but in the universe.

· · · · ·

## 4. Awareness

The word *awareness* gets thrown around in new age circles like it's a party trick everyone wants to learn. The quest for enlightenment or awakening consumes many an ego, turning people into show-boating seekers, all with higher states of awareness. Visit any new age store or event, and someone in the room will be boasting about their level of awareness. They will have a long list of party tricks they can do that they need to tell you about. The problem is what people do is not who they are. Doing is not being, and being is where the awareness is. Awareness answers the big life question "Who am I, and why am I here?" Read that again. Really read it, and see that nowhere in that question does it ask, "What do I do?" The truth is it's easier to list party tricks than it is to spend deep and meaningful time getting to know yourself, which is why most people who love to wax lyrical about their level of awareness aren't very aware at all.

My experience in new age circles has been very similar to my experience of high school and office environments. The loudest people in the room are normally the ones with the most fear in their hearts. Awareness means having an understanding, a form of consciousness, an act of realization, and the ability to grasp or understand a situation or experience. In other words, it's about knowing what's going on from moment to moment and the part you play, or don't play, in that moment's unfolding.

Most people aren't aware. This is not a criticism, but it is true. Most people are too caught up in their heads and their own inner voices to really notice what is happening around them. Count how many times you hear the phrase "I was unaware" or "I had no idea." You will be surprised how often you hear it. People with expanded levels of awareness can read a room, can assess situations quickly, and understand how interactions cause chain reactions. Awareness is nothing but mental training, and it is less a spiritual practice and more a choice we make. It is something that we train our mind to do through practice and discipline. The stronger and healthier the lower chakras are, the easier our awareness practice becomes. That is what it truly is—a crown chakra practice, and one that starts and ends with the question "Who am I, and why am I here?"

## EXERCISE

. . . . .

In the tarot, we already have cards that show us what it means to dedicate one's life to a disciplined practice: the knights. Each of the knights practices in different areas. The Knight of Cups is practicing emotional awareness, the Knight of Swords is practicing mental awareness, the Knight of Wands is practicing spiritual awareness, and the Knight of Pentacles is practicing physical awareness. Combined, the knights of the tarot show us the many facets of our own awareness training and practice. Awareness is not singular in its nature; rather, it is all encompassing. Once we find out in the pages that awareness is a practice, the majority of us spend our lives working at the level of the knights. Very few people make it to king level of awareness. We can probably count the number of truly awakened, aware, and enlightened people in the world right now on our fingers. That is how few of them there are.

With this in mind, it is time for you to select your significator card from the four tarot knights. I recommend you do this blindly, and by that I mean shuffle your four knights, place them face down so you can't see them, and then select one and flip it over. Let your intuition guide you to the aspect of your awareness that needs to be worked on, strengthened, and practiced.

Once you have your card, take it to your journal and start by writing whether or not receiving this card was a surprise or expected. Then move into asking your knight what sort of practice you should be doing. Remember, knights are all about daily training, as they are constantly sharpening their skills and expanding their awareness of the space around them, while also stilling and settling the space inside of them. Your tarot knight has a training regimen that they are just itching to share with you, one that will strengthen your awareness in the area of your knight's domain and harness the energy of your lower chakras. It might help if you can imagine your tarot knight actively walking you through a training session. Imagine the clothes you are wearing, the tools the knight hands you or instructs you in using, the movements, the words, the colors, and the smells. Expand your five senses as you imagine this session and write down every detail. Perhaps your knight has some mantras to teach you, some fancy footwork, or maybe even some Jedi mind tricks. Whatever it is, write it all down.

When you have finished your training session, pick up your favorite tarot books and see what other information you can find out about your knight. Remember to keep your research content specific, so be on the lookout for crown chakra words like *understanding, recognition, knowledge, consciousness, intuition, insight, mindfulness*, and, of course, *awareness*. The more you know about how your tarot knight connects to your crown chakra and your center of awareness, the easier it will be to train with them, practice with them, and accept them as your mentor and partner along the path of your self-actualization journey. Who knows, maybe through all of this you might even get a flicker of who you are and why you are here.

· · · · ·

## 5. Wisdom

Wisdom is one of those concepts whose location is actually hard to identify. I have placed it here in the crown because I believe the crown chakra is the meeting point of the three brains, which are the gut, the heart, and the mind. These three brains all collect and process information, and they all send it into the crown, which then sends selected parts of that information out to the corresponding chakras and body parts. Wisdom is a deep understanding of not just the information itself but how we use it, when we use it, and why we use it in our everyday lives. A collection of information is knowledge, but putting it into practice is wisdom. Wisdom is gained through trial and error, which means to become wise one must know not only what it means to succeed, but also what it means to fail. One also needs to know what it means to gain and what it means to let go of, or lose, and understand that either side of the coin is beneficial. Wisdom is understanding that actions have consequences, but sometimes you have to hedge your bets on however those consequences play out. In this respect, wisdom connects the heart and the solar plexus to the crown in a triangle of thoughts, feelings, and actions. This is not the neatest triangle in the world, and the connecting lines look more like someone plotting the course of the planets over the night sky, but then again wisdom isn't exactly linear.

We can be wise in some areas before we are wise in others. Some things need age and time, while others we have carried with us for multiple lifetimes, and sometimes we are born with wisdom beyond our numbered years. It is often the wisdom we are born with that we fight against the most. This wisdom is deeply connected to our soul and its purpose for this particular incarnation, as it is a form of consciousness that drives a lot of our core desires—and ones that may seem out of alignment with the plans of those around you. This soul wisdom is divine, and it draws its power straight from the heart and the connection energy the crown chakra has with the universe. This soul wisdom has been trying to burst forth since the moment you were born. It has been stalking you, haunting your dreams, and whispering in your ear from your very first breath. It is this soul wisdom we are going to focus on for the remainder of this section, as this is the strongest wisdom you carry with you. The other type of wisdom is learned from living a long life. Life wisdom takes time and is bound to the karmic lessons you have yet to clear. Soul wisdom is wisdom you have now. It is at your fingertips, ready and waiting to make positive enhancements to the way you live your life, the way you feel about your life, and the way you think about why you are here right now in this time, in this body, and in this ancestral line.

## EXERCISE
· · · · ·

To find a significator for this part of the crown chakra, you are going to do an intuitive draw from the court cards only, and the reason for this is that none of us know exactly how old our soul is. It ages differently from our physical body. Soul lives are more cyclic than linear, and we want to know what wisdom you have in your current soul cycle. The court cards are the go-to cards for stages of cycles. They show us the four stages of progress we make inside a single cycle, starting at the page and working our way up to king. This makes them the perfect cards to help us find both your soul cycle and the wisdom it is offering you for this particular time in your life. So, remove the sixteen court cards from your deck and shuffle them slowly and gently, as you imagine a golden light like sunshine coming down through your crown. Feel this warm light energy as it moves into your arms and makes its way down to your fingers. Watch as this golden light starts to infuse with the cards themselves, infusing them with this energy from your higher self. Once the cards feel totally infused with this golden sunlight energy, fan them out in front of you face down. Place your hands in a prayer position and hold them to your heart as you take three nice, long, deep breaths, and ask, "What soul wisdom is needing to burst forth at this time?" Repeat the question three times, as it helps focus the mind and the energy of the cards.

When you feel ready, select your card. Keep in mind these cards represent the stages in a cycle, so first let's identify what stage you are in. If it is a page, you are in a new soul cycle, which means the wisdom you are bringing forth is about beginnings, starting over, or starting something new for the very first time. This shows you have the innate wisdom to make this leap of faith. If you turned over a knight, it means you are in the hard work part of your cycle, building habits, setting goals, and engaging in a lot of action. The wisdom you are drawing on here is resilience, persistence, and commitment, which shows that at this time, you have the stamina inside you to stick with whatever goal or dream you have been working on. If you have selected a queen, then this shows a particularly social part of your cycle, and even if you are an introvert, you will have wisdom available to you right now to discern which social settings are to your soul's benefit and which ones you can graciously decline.

This is the first step in reclaiming your soul power. It is the first dance with leadership, and in many ways, it is the first time you will have been taken seriously as a thought leader or spiritual teacher. If you selected a king, then it is time to lead, to step into a role that you have been grooming yourself for over the course of many lifetimes. Stepping into this role will mean sharing your wisdom with others, trusting your wisdom, and walking an authentic path with your wisdom. In other words, it's time to live your soul's truth, with no more hiding, no more excuses, and no more shrugging off your responsibilities.

There is much to learn from your court card and many discussions you can have with this card inside your journal. Keep in mind that the wisdom this soul cycle offers is also important to your healing journey. This wisdom could very well be the cure for old wounds and the liberator of old illness patterns. The more you work with this card as your soul wisdom significator, the more will be revealed.

· · · · ·

## 6. Potential

My coach tells me all the time that what we can be is linked to why we are here, which shows us that potential is about being, which often causes us to do amazing things. This makes sense when we remember that the crown chakra is not a doing center but a being center. However, that doesn't make it any easier to wrap one's head around, especially when you are a doer, you push your limits through doing, and, therefore, you have your potential linked to that doing. Bringing potential into the crown chakra and understanding that our true nature, our true potential, is not at all what we do is a totally different way to view who we are and why we are here. We answer the question "Why am I here?" by just being. I guess an easier way to come at this might be from the perspective that one's gift is actually one's potential or one's reason to be here. For some, it is numbers and mathematics; for others it is words and writing; for others it is law, medicine, or childcare. We could not be anyone else except for who our gift and potential drives us to be. Potential is something we know, just like how we know to breathe. We just do it, and we could do it in our sleep. Potential is something so deep in us that we don't even really have to think about it. You could even say your potential is instinctual.

However, that still doesn't mean you will ever reach it. Humans have a tendency to make things complex. They can take the simplest of tasks and make it extraordinarily difficult, which is why some people never seem to grow into their potential and never truly understand why they are here. Instead, they can become seduced by the more laborious and harder path of doing, which can lead to the vicious cycle of constantly measuring our self-worth and our reason for existing against other people's accomplishments. This takes the energy away from the crown chakra, the chakra open to and linked to higher vibrations and unlimited energy, and places potential down in the lower chakras, among the limited physical energy. Taking your potential, which thrives with direct access to universal energy, and placing it closer to the heavier, earth-based energy could constrict and make your potential struggle. It is much harder for that potential to grow, as first it needs to make it all the way back to the crown chakra. It needs to be in the right set of conditions so it can thrive and bloom.

Really, that is the perfect way to visualize your unique potential: to see it as the unfolding lotus at the top of your crown. The more you relax into just being, the more petals unfurl and spread their beautiful color. This gorgeous flower basks in the light of the divine. It needs that light to live, and as it fills up with this energy, it sends it back to you via the roots it has embedded deep in your crown chakra. The energy of unlimited potential flows down your entire chakra system, making you feel whole, clear, certain, loved, worthy, filled with desire, and safe. This is what true potential feels like. It is a connection to something beyond this physical experience. It is energy that is complete and without need. It is something we struggle with here in a world of things, wants, and limitation.

## EXERCISE
· · · · ·

What is your potential? Are you allowing yourself to connect with it, or are you drowning it in a sea of doing?

Selecting a significator for this part of your crown chakra may be somewhat challenging, as you are going to need to look for cards that aren't active. You are going to have to search for cards that best represent someone just being, or maybe look for passive cards in the deck and select from those. Recommended cards are the Star, the Moon, the Sun, the World, the aces, the Four of Swords, the Seven of Pentacles, the Two of Wands, the Three of Wands, and the Nine of Cups.

When you take this particular card to your journal, start with the question "How does this card help me unlock the riddle of why I am here?" Start by just examining the artwork on your card. Each deck is different, and your card may have something in the artwork that triggers you to start writing. It might be a symbol or a specific item. Perhaps the figure in your card is drawn a specific way, like a fairy, goddess, or an animal. Does that add or subtract from the answer you seek? Keep exploring the artwork until you have nothing left to say, and then move on to the meaning of the card itself. If you have a working knowledge of this card, start there. If not, pick up your favorite tarot books and search for key words or phrases that are specific to potential, remembering to always keep your research on topic, no matter how tempting it is to stray.

Take this one step further by pairing this card up with your clarity significator. Use the magical pairs exercises we have used elsewhere in this book to explore how your potential and your clarity work hand in hand. Start by putting the potential card before the clarity card, and then switch them. This will show you how these two chakras work together to steer you along your path. You will also see how when you are connected to the vibrational universe, how much clearer your sight will be. If you want, add one more card and take this from a magical pairs exercise to a three-card spread by adding your safety significator card, and laying your cards out as such:

- *Card 1:* Potential Significator
- *Card 2:* Clarity Significator
- *Card 3:* Safety Significator

These three cards will give you a wonderful visual of what it means to be tapped in (root chakra), tuned in (third eye chakra), and turned on (crown chakra), not to mention it will once again remind you that no chakra is an island. They are all connected and rely on one another to fully function. By all means, use your journal to explore your magical pairs and the three-card spread.

· · · · ·

## 7. Inspiration

In a world of noisy ideas and people desperate to be heard, it can be impossible to hear the whispers of inspiration. Inspiration is quick and sure, yet gentle and quiet. Inspiration is a flash, and it is often-times intangible, which makes it difficult to hold on to. It is a brief encounter with the heart, the mind, and the Divine that takes place in your crown chakra. Inspiration is more of a feeling than it is a thought. The energy that pumps through the brain turns it into a thought, so it is more understandable and accessible. Even then, most of us miss inspiration, as it gently blows across the surface of our conscious mind.

Thankfully, inspiration is constantly chatting to us. It never goes away, and it is always willing to dialogue, ready and waiting when we are. The problem is that we are very rarely ready to get caught up with inspiration. Like most energy in the crown, inspiration does not know limitation, nor does it care much for the workings of the phys-ical world. It is larger than life, and it will always give us a glimpse of a life bigger than the one we are currently living. This scares people more than it excites them, as not everyone is ready or willing to push themselves into the grander vision inspiration brings with it. Hence, this is why ideas are often favored over inspiration.

Ideas seem manageable. They feel controllable, and, of course, they are easier to map, track, and contain. Living an inspired life, on the other hand, is like constantly walking in the Fool's shoes, never quite knowing what's going to happen or how things are going to turn out, but happy to take the journey all the same. In fact, if ever there was a significator for this section of the crown chakra, it would be the Fool, and that is the card you will be working with for the remainder of this section. This is ironic, because this is the last stop on the chakra pillar, but the Fool is the starting point of the tarot journey. Perhaps the Fool is teaching us how to engage with this energy, as if we are at the beginning of an adventure, because to be honest, that is what living an inspired life is. It is adventurous. The Fool in the tarot encapsulates a certain amount of vulnerability in naivety. This translates into great courage and a certain amount of stubbornness, for one has to be somewhat immovable when it comes to following inspiration. This means you can't be easily talked out of your adventure, and the Fool is all that and more.

## EXERCISE
· · · · ·

To really see how this adventurous spirit is playing out in your life, pair your Fool card with your heart chakra significator and do the magical pairs exercise. These two cards work hand in hand all day, every day, and throughout your nighttime dreams. They are constantly chatting, working on ways to push you into your soul version, and finding new and creative ways to make you explore your unlimited potential. Do this exercise with the Fool in the first position and the heart chakra significator in the second position. Journal on this for as long as you can, and if you feel the need, pick up your favorite tarot book and look for descriptive words or phrases related to inspiration in regard to the magical pair you have in front of you.

Next, put your heart significator back in the deck and place your Fool card where you can see it. Pick up your tarot deck and begin to shuffle slowly and gently as you gaze at your Fool card, and then draw one card for each of the following questions:

- *Card 1:* How can inspiration help me with my job or career?
- *Card 2:* How can inspiration assist me in deepening my relationships at home?
- *Card 3:* In what way does inspiration show up in my everyday life?
- *Card 4:* What next inspired step will assist me with my healing journey?
- *Card 5:* How can I be more open to inspiration?
- *Card 6:* What fear is currently blocking my inspiration?
- *Card 7:* What is stopping me right now from living an inspired life?
- *Card 8:* How can I step into the shoes of the Fool?

Once you have all eight cards drawn and laid out in a row in front of you, take notice if you have any recurring numbers or suits, as this may indicate your inspirational preferred element or number energy, with which you can dialogue. Place them together as a group, as we don't need to read these cards in the order they were drawn. Grouping them will in fact give you more information. Identify any reversed cards and group them together as well. What about court cards or major arcana cards? If you have a few of those, put the majors in one group and the courts in another.

You are going to read your groups after you take a look at the single cards still laid out in front of you. Take any and all cards that did not make it into a group, line them up in a row, and read them as a spread, as if this line is a story straight from your inspiration. Open your journal and write about this story, even if it is only one sentence or a couple of key words.

Next, move on to the groups. It doesn't matter where you start, just slowly work your way around each group or magical pair you have collected and talk about how these cards are answering the questions. I know we have taken them out of order, and mixed them up with answers from other questions, but that is rather the point. Inspiration is not linear, and it pulls information from all areas in order to provide you with answers and flashes of life-changing opportunities. Each group or magical pair can be used to answer all the above questions.

Don't worry if you find this challenging at first, as it takes time to get used to the disorganized, nonlinear dialoguing process of inspiration. Sometimes it seems simple, and other times it is frustrating and almost impossible to make sense of, so don't rush this. Take as much time as you want. You might take a few days to go through the entire eight cards. However long it takes you is the perfect amount of time. The important thing is not the time it takes you to dialogue with the cards, but the dialogue itself, as this is a conscious conversation you are having with your inspiration via your tarot cards. Keep this dialogue up for as long as you can. This will bring your inspiration's voice, its whispers, to the forefront of your awareness. Perhaps next time, it won't be quite so hard to hear it over all the other noise inside your head.

· · · · ·

## Crown Chakra Tarot Healing

Now that you have worked through the seven key issues of the seventh chakra, it is time to do some energy healing work on all that you have discovered, all that has bubbled up, and all that has presented itself for cleaning and clearing. Grab your tarot deck and get out the significator cards for the issues covered in this chapter. Select your significator card for the crown chakra and place it in front of you. This card is going to be the middle card in your crown chakra healing mandala wheel.

Your card order is as follows:

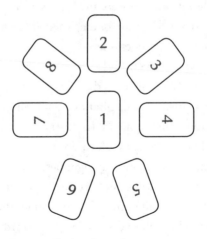

- *Card 1:* Crown Chakra Significator
- *Card 2:* Connection Significator
- *Card 3:* Divinity Significator
- *Card 4:* Wholeness Significator

- *Card 5:* Awareness Significator
- *Card 6:* Wisdom Significator
- *Card 7:* Potential Significator
- *Card 8:* Inspiration Significator

Your center card is going to be the energy you will see flowing in and out of the other cards, as if a beautiful purple-gold smoke wisps out of the card and starts to tickle the other cards around it. As we move into the visualization part of this exercise, move your hands over the cards as you say the following affirmations for each of the cards surrounding your crown chakra significator. The tarot mandala helps anchor your energy healing work and allows you to engage more fully with the overall process. Your affirmations are as follows:

- *Card 2:* I am connected to the energy of the universe.
- *Card 3:* I am the divine made flesh and bone.
- *Card 4:* I am complete and whole when I am one with all parts of myself.
- *Card 5:* I am constantly expanding my awareness so I can better serve myself and others.
- *Card 6:* I am stepping into the wise part of who I am and acknowledging its existence.
- *Card 7:* I am learning to question the limits I have placed around my potential.
- *Card 8:* I am allowing myself to step into the Fool's shoes more often so I can learn to live a more inspired life.

Find somewhere comfortable and quiet, where you won't be disturbed for up to twenty minutes. Place your cards where you can see them and start rubbing your palms gently together as you focus on your breathing. Rub your hands together for about forty seconds, activating the energy centers in your palms. You might start to feel some heat in your hands, and this is good. Now place your hands over your crown or rest them on top of your head and focus on your breath, inhaling through your nose. Feel the breath as it hits the back of your throat, fills your lungs, and expands your chest. As you exhale from the mouth, feel the breath leaving your body and deflating the lungs. Let the breath work become automatic, and shift your focus to your cards, starting with the center card, which is your crown chakra significator. Visualize the purple-gold smoke gently rising from the card and twirling around the wheel you have created around it. Each time you exhale, the smoky wisps extend farther and farther. Sit like this for a few minutes, just doing the breath work and keeping your hands on your crown area as you feel your chest rise and fall, and visualize the smoky purple-gold energy infusing your spread.

When you feel ready, move your hands to your tarot mandala and move them along each card as you speak the corresponding affirmation statements out loud. Read through the entire list three times. Once you have finished, just relax and focus on the breath work, placing the hands back over your crown. As you inhale, feel the smoky purple-gold energy coming into your nose, sending it up to the crown and infusing the crown chakra. Relax into this, as you inhale all this lovely infused energy, letting it clean and clear your crown chakra as it embeds your affirmations into your chakra. When this feels complete, remove your hands and just breathe normally for thirty to forty seconds. Thank your cards, and you are done.

You can repeat this simple tarot healing session anytime you want, and by all means, journal about how the session made you feel or any revelations you had during the session. The more you know, the more you inquire, the more you heal.

# 8

# Pulling It All Together

Throughout this book you have gathered a lot of information about your chakras, and while this amount of information is not something that you need to do on a regular basis, this deep dive into your chakras is something I recommend doing a couple of times a year as you continue on your healing journey. I also recommend that you check on your chakras monthly and do a mini diagnostic dialogue. I suggest that you pick one issue per chakra and create a monthly chakra pillar spread, focused on whatever you have going on for that month. Perhaps, you will be traveling, or maybe you are winding up a big project. Pick out the issues from the seven chakra chapters that would align with the energy you will either be working with or need to tap into to stabilize, empower, and draw upon. Essentially, you will create a monthly seven-card spread that will set the tone for your month and help hold sacred space for your energetic body.

Let me provide you with an example:

## Chakra Pillar for Travel for Business Trips, Conferences, and Conventions

For many of us, traveling for our work is common. We find ourselves heading to events, retreats, workshops, conferences, or conventions a couple of times a year. If you know that this is your month to travel, you may wish to use this chakra pillar spread to help hold the space for the trip and help the energetic body with all the new energies it will undoubtedly come into contact with. For this spread, you can either pull the cards deliberately, so that you are infusing a very specific energy into your travel, or you can do it intuitively, so you can allow your intention to guide you. Trust that whichever way you decided to approach pulling the cards is the most perfect way for you. Here are your card associations:

- *Card 7:* Crown Chakra, Connection
- *Card 6:* Third Eye, Intuition
- *Card 5:* Throat Chakra, Hearing and Being Heard
- *Card 4:* Heart Chakra, Fellowship
- *Card 3:* Solar Plexus Chakra, Engagement
- *Card 2:* Sacral Chakra, Pleasure
- *Card 1:* Root Chakra, Safety

With the above cards, you can see we are already setting the stage to have a pleasurable and engaging experience in which we will feel safe and supported, while creating a space of open and authentic dialogue between ourselves and all those we will meet along the path of our journey. You can do this with anything that is coming up for you throughout the year. You can leave these cards up on your altar for the month, and use them as part of your meditation process, or you could take a picture of them, print them, and place them in your journal or daily planner so you can reference the spread throughout your travels. It is entirely up to you to decide which approach best suits your needs. Just know it is a fabulous and quick way to keep up the ongoing dialogue with your chakras on a regular basis.

## How to Use This Book as Part of Your Daily Energy Work Practice

Now that you have completed this book, I encourage you not to put it on a shelf and be done with it. Rather, I offer up a way for you to use this book as a part of your daily healing practice. It could be as simple as closing your eyes and holding this book to your heart chakra while you take a few deep breaths and flipping to a page somewhere in the book. Use that page as your cue for which chakra and which issue want to play with you and your cards that day. Draw a single card and see what the message is. This simple use of the book in conjunction with your cards and chakra system will keep the doors of communication open between the three of you, not to mention it will allow you a casual, playful way to engage with your energy body on a daily basis. If you want to go further, you can use the book-flipping method and pull three cards, asking deeper questions. These questions might include "What does this chakra issue want me to know today?," "How does it want me to work with it today?," and "What action can I take to deepen my relationship with this issue inside my energetic body?" How you allocate the cards and design the spread is entirely up to you. Maybe you like a four- or five-card spread and want to pull more cards to get a bigger view of the message. That works too. The most important thing is to make it fit to your daily tarot practice.

We have also utilized journaling as an effective tool throughout the book to gain further insights and to deepen our awareness of ourselves and the healing process. I recommend that you continue to integrate journaling with your daily chakra draw. While its use in your daily chakra work may be much simpler and quicker, it can still be an invaluable tool. Perhaps you already know what chakra you want to work with. Close your eyes, take a moment to connect with it, ask a question that is relevant for your day, pull a card (or two or ten), and then move into your journal and see what information the chakra and cards have for your question.

Let me give you an example: Perhaps you have been having digestive issues, and you want to open a dialogue with your solar plexus to see what is going on. Take a moment to settle in, close your eyes, take some deep breaths, and imagine a yellow light just above your belly button. Once you have established your connection, ask your question to the solar plexus. The question may be "Solar plexus, you seem out of sorts, so how can I be of service today?" Next, pull your card or cards. These cards will answer your question, so take them to your journal and spend some time with them. See if they bring up issues that you can identify in the book, even if they are not part of the solar plexus chapter. This may be a hint at where the issue is stemming from, as most times where a problem shows up is not always where you need to be directing the healing. It might take a while to get used to using the cards and the book in this way, but stick with it, as I guarantee that you will reap the rewards of your persistence.

Of course, it goes without saying: *never, ever use the cards or this book in place of medical advice.* If something is seriously wrong with your physical body, consult a medical professional immediately.

# A Word for Energy Workers: Taking This Work into Your Practice and Using It on Others

For the most part, this book is written for self-healing. It is put together so that you, the reader, can take your own journey through the chakras, get to know your personal chakra system, and refine the way you work and dialogue with your chakra system. However, that is only one way you can use the contents of this book. If you are a reiki practitioner, Healing Touch worker, massage therapist, or any other energy healer, you may wish to use what you have learned in this book with your own clients. I highly encourage you to find a way to integrate the *Tarot Healer* work within your own specialized area of expertise, which is why I have devised a simple framework to begin this collaboration of modalities.

The first thing I recommend is to do the chakra pillar exercise at the very start of this book with your client, as you want a fresh snapshot of what is going on in all seven of the chakras. This tarot chakra pillar will allow you to pinpoint areas that are of concern and zero in on them. Make sure you do this with cards upside down and read them as if they are in the protective aspect, meaning each card will show an energy being protected inside each of the chakras. Be on the lookout for cards that show change (Tower, Chariot, and any of the fives), anxiety (the Moon, the Devil, the Nine of Swords, Two of Pentacles, and the Seven of Wands), stuck or blocked energy (Death, the Four of Pentacles, the Two of Swords, the Eight of Swords, and the Ten of Wands), and cards that show endings, grief, and sorrow (the Three of Swords, the Five of Cups, the Ten of Swords, the World, the Eight of Cups). These cards are the ones you want to focus on first, slowly refining these seemingly problematic energies even more until you decide which chakra is in need of a much closer look.

This is where you would move into that chakra's chapter and start creating a chakra mandala for your client. This will help narrow the issue within that particular chakra. You will be able to identify one or more concerns your client has within the chakra itself. This takes your healing work to a whole new level, especially when your client gets to see the cards that represent each of these issues.

If you want to go even deeper still, you can create a healing mandala for just the main issue that is causing the problem. This can be done by placing the issue significator into the middle of the mandala and drawing seven cards to correspond to the issues inside of that chakra. This shows you how this one main issue is affecting all the other areas of that particular chakra. This is often one of the most powerful visual exercises you can do with your clients, as you have taken them on a journey from big picture to micro picture. You started with the entire chakra system, and now you are just looking at one issue inside one chakra as the focus of your healing work. Seeing how the cards pull this energy down to one small issue will allow your client to see their energy bodies in a totally different way. You can dialogue with your client and ask them questions about the image of the card and how it makes them feel.

This interactive approach helps your clients feel more a part of the process of their healing. As the healer, this allows you to tailor your work with your client to really dig in and do some laser-focused clearing work in that chakra. This framework is how I personally approach it, but it is not the only way. The more comfortable you become with the chakras and all their many issues and concerns, the more refined and creative your individual approach will become. Allow this book to guide you to new and different ways to deepen your work with your clients.

# Conclusion

Well, dear reader, we have come to the end of our journey together. You have worked hard, and I am proud of you. Taking this sort of healing journey is not for the faint of heart. Give yourself and your chakras a high five! I would also love to hear your experiences of this book and if you are indeed using it in your healing practice with your clients. Drop me a line on social media or email me directly at leezarobertsontarot@gmail.com.

# Recommended Reading

Beckwith, Bernard Michael. *Life Visioning: A Transformative Process for Activating Your Unique Gifts and Highest Potential.* Boulder, CO: Sounds True, 2012.

Brown, Brené. *Rising Strong as a Spiritual Practice.* Louisville, CO: Sounds True, 2017. Audiobook.

Choquette, Sonia. *Your 3 Best Super Powers: Meditation, Imagination & Intuition.* Carlsbad, CA: Hay House, 2016.

Dalai Lama, Desmond Tutu, and Carlton Douglas Abrams. *The Book of Joy: Lasting Happiness in a Changing World.* New York: Avery, 2016.

Dyer, Wayne. *Excuse Begone!: How to Change Lifelong, Self-Defeating Thinking Habits.* Carlsbad, CA: Hay House, 2009.

Jagat, Guru. *Invincible Living: The Power of Yoga, the Energy of Breath, and Other Tools for a Radiant Life.* San Francisco, CA: HarperOne, 2017.

Katie, Byron, and Stephen Mitchell. *A Mind at Home with Itself: How Asking Four Questions Can Free Your Mind, Open Your Heart, and Turn Your World Around.* New York: HarperOne, 2017.

Kondo, Marie. *The Life-Changing Magic of Tidying Up: The Japanese Art of Decluttering and Organizing*. Berkeley, CA: Ten Speed Press, 2014.

LaPorte, Danielle. *White Hot Truth: Clarity for Keeping It Real on Your Spiritual Path from One Seeker to Another*. Vancouver, CA: Virtuonica, 2017.

Len, Ihaleakala Hew, and Joe Vitale. *Zero Limits: The Secret Hawaiian System for Health, Wealth, Peace and More*. Hoboken, NJ: Wiley, 2007.

Peer, Marisa. *I Am Enough: Mark Your Mirror and Change Your Life*. Self-published, 2018.

# Bibliography

Jagat, Guru. *Invincible Living: The Power of Yoga, the Energy of Breath, and Other Tools for a Radiant Life.* San Francisco, CA: HarperOne, 2017.

Jobs, Steve. "Steve Jobs: The Next Insanely Great Thing." Interview by Gary Wolf. *Wired*, February 1, 1996. https://www.wired.com /1996/02/jobs-2/.

Katie, Byron, and Stephen Mitchell. *A Mind at Home with Itself: How Asking Four Questsions Can Free Your Mind, Open Your Heart, and Turn Your Worldd Around.* New York: HarperOne, 2017.

Len, Ihaleakala Hew, and Joe Vitale. *Zero Limits: The Secret Hawaiian System for Health, Wealth, Peace and More.* Hoboken, NJ: Wiley, 2007.

Levitt, Steven, and Stephen J. Dubner. *Freakonomics.* New York: HarperCollins, 2005.

Patel, Alpa V., Maret L. Maliniak, Erika Rees-Punia, Charles E. Matthews, and Susan M. Gapstur. "Prolonged Leisure Time Spent Sitting in Relation to Cause-Specific Mortality in a Large US Cohort." *American Journal of Epidemiology* 187, no.

10 (October 2018): 2,151–58. https://doi.org/10.1093/aje
/kwy125.

Peer, Marisa. "Do This to Completely HEAL Your Mind and
Body," MindValley Talks, September 6, 2019, YouTube video,
51:39, https://www.youtube.com/watch?v=egbiGhAiN8E&
feature=youtu.be.

———. *I Am Enough: Mark Your Mirror and Change Your Life.*
Self-published, 2018.

Robbins, Mel. *The 5 Second Rule: Transform Your Life, Work, and
Confidence with Everyday Courage.* Self-published, Savio Republic, 2017.

"The Science of HeartMath." HeartMath. Accessed January 15,
2020. https://www.heartmath.com/science.